"It is no exaggeration to say that, over the past four months, since I started working with Deborah, I have been reborn. I think that originally, almost 70 years ago, I was born depressed. In my baby pictures, I look like I carried the weight of the world on my shoulders. I spent more years in, and money on, traditional therapy than I care to remember. I was diagnosed—PTSD, chronic low mood, and worst of all, 'dispirited.' I experienced addiction. During therapy, painful memories surfaced, along with extreme anxiety and panic attacks, for which I received medication. Therapy was helpful, but I continued to struggle with 'chronic low mood.' I had a good life. but something was missing. Where was the joy, the passion for life? I felt I was just going through the motions. I always saw myself as Eeyore in *Winnie the Pooh*—under a dark cloud of depression. In May of this year, I began attending Deborah's meditation group. As a result of what I was experiencing during meditation, I began to see Deborah for spiritual counseling and energy healing. I have been astounded! So much negative energy has been released in these sessions—almost 70 years' worth! For the first time in my life, I feel free of psychic pain! I am feeling joyful, and look forward to each day. I can feel and accept love from my friends and am pursuing new interests with excitement I didn't know was possible. Most of all I feel the Presence of the divine—the G[o]od in the Universe and know that this Presence is part of me. (OK, Deborah—it *is* me.) Sometimes I feel such love and joy that I think I might burst with it! I am truly grateful and blessed. Thank you, Deborah."

~ Chris Tupper Bibby, retired Geriatric Social Worker

"She is my beloved teacher. She guided me to the light and I was able to accomplish a lot. I am seeing her regularly, once or twice a month. It is the most valuable time that I give myself. I look forward to it, always."

~ Junga Yoon, Residential Counselor
at a Mental Health Program

"For whatever reason, God (or the innate, universal intelligence of the universe) has put you in my thoughts for a while now. I really just wanted to say hi and thank you. I'm currently (over the past year and a half) in a life-forming transformational stage. Call it faith and truly listening and seeing signs on an almost daily basis of where my life should go, or better yet, where *I* wanted my life to go. We truly have guardian angels watching over us and we can communicate if we can listen still enough. And I never would be here if it wasn't for you, truly. Love you always."

~ Dr. Brian J. Trudnak, Chiropractic Physician

"You have helped me grow and develop as a more loving and conscious person. You showed up as a mothering presence that fostered a God understanding that was not offered through blood relations. You offered me focus and direction of the heart instead of the head. You still do, every time we sit together, your own life's experience and faith are shared and help me find clarity in my own. I get to be a pupil of Deb's school of faith, integrity, and love. Reminding me what God really is and teaching me to see It, and have a relationship with It myself."

~ Jaqueline Traci Bosley, Dog Groomer, Reiki Master, Arborist Assistant, Artist

---

"When I met Deborah in January of 2012, my previously flourishing career was floundering, my personal and professional relationships were in a state of turmoil and I was diagnosed with a debilitating autoimmune disease. I was angry, resentful, afraid, and most of all, utterly exhausted. The more I fought to get well, improve relationships, and address issues in my career, the worse things became. Though much of that time is a blur of stress, illness, and exhaustion, I clearly remember a friend suggesting I contact Deborah. I did and what followed was nothing short of a miracle.

I can only describe my sessions with Deborah as a light switch flipping on. Everything had seemed so dark and hopeless and then 'flip'—the light came on. I was able to see and feel the joy and blessings in life.

Even after just one session, my diagnosis and situation were the same upon leaving as it was when I arrived—yet it was also completely different, full of hope. After working with Deborah for less than four months, I was in complete remission, harmony had been restored to my relationships and my career was back on track; I had found my dream job. Every session leaves you in a state of relaxed alignment that is hard to describe but miraculous to experience. While every session varies in a multitude of ways, the constant is that you always get what you need and leave feeling a combination of joy, peace, vibrancy, and wellness.

Meeting with Deborah is like conversing with a beloved, a lifelong friend that knows all your faults and loves you anyway *and* a visit to an attentive and knowledgeable physician *and* a session with a talented, intuitive, caring therapist, *all at once.*

I still am not sure I accurately described the amazingness of it all!"

~ Sara Hoomis-Tracy, Elementary School Principal

"I have been blessed to know Deborah Evans Hogan for over 20 years. I have referred Deborah to many of my inner circle loved ones for her healing and direct communication with The Divine. What I love about her way of healing is her grounding presence, unconditional love, and honesty. She is so grounded! My friends and family have loved their sessions with her. Her ability to communicate with those who have passed is amazing. She has gifted my loved ones with clarity and healing."

~ Shauna Hubley, Director of Operations
for a Software Company

"Deborah is my friend, my mentor, my minister... she is amazing... you will learn so much from her, mostly, that you have all the knowledge you need, if you just stop and listen."

~ Gail LaPointe, RN

"Absolutely life-changing. My journey with Deborah started in 2011 when I met her at my school when she came to do an introduction on Energy Work. I took her Reiki I class shortly after.

Fast-forward to 2014. My father passed away. I was distraught. I ran into Deborah in a supermarket parking lot days after his passing. I had learned she just moved to the area where I lived. Coincidence? Maybe.

Fast-forward again to 2018. I was completely broken. I endured two severely abusive relationships and had a warped relationship with my family. I was lost, scared, confused, and desperate. I remembered Deborah and reached out to her. She got me into her healing room right away and since that very day, I have experienced a transition of life that I never thought was possible for myself. A life I never thought I deserved. I went from a 27-year-old who had no idea what life was, who was untrusting, angry, and tired, to a thriving 30-year-old, who is now engaged to a wonderful man and living on our own farm with many animals—a dream I've had since I was nine years old. I have now learned that *everything* has a reason, and I am *completely* responsible for how I choose to live my life regardless of all the unfortunate experiences that have happened. I have been able to backtrack on many experiences in my life and put the puzzle pieces together for my own understanding and closure. It is so freeing.

Running into Deborah days after my father's death was not a coincidence. It simply set the stage for what was to come. I am not afraid of my PTSD anymore. I speak freely of it and I willingly and proudly tell my story in hopes it may inspire others. I have improved my communication skills, which was something I always struggled with. And I have greatly repaired the relationship with my mother. These are all just a few of the *many* things Deborah has helped me with.

Deborah's loving care has guided me in finding and trusting Spirit. To always know and believe that everything works out just as it should if you choose to allow it. Deborah has taught me that I can achieve anything I desire - possibilities are endless when I trust and believe in myself and Spirit.

My work with Deborah has also resulted in my business thriving. Thriving so much that I have now taken on the role of helping those who have struggled to find their own successes. Deborah has always told me that she envisioned me becoming an educator, on business and in life support for others who may have had similar challenges. She was right (as always!). Just recently I was approached by someone extremely well known in my industry. They asked me to create a seminar on operating businesses successfully!

I am so thankful for Deborah, her devotion to helping her students heal and grow, and for quite literally, saving my life. I love you, Deborah! Thank you for everything, you are amazing!"

~ Casey Mabardy, Holistic Dog Grooming Salon Owner

"Deborah has helped me to see that faith will guide you exactly where you want to go. That thought of not being enough is just fear lying to you. I am becoming faster to recognize this through my work with her. She has helped me sustain myself in a place where I'm open to receiving, open to love, and open to trust that everything truly does happen just as it should and always for my greater good.

My life has changed and the gentle steering (meaning the regular spiritual ass-kicking) and support have created a knowing that everything is always working out.

Thank you for always going above and beyond to help me grow."

~ Lisa Gagnon, Retail Management

If you truly love nature,
you will find beauty everywhere.

~ Vincent van Gogh

Mystical Partnership

Extraordinary Experiences
of an Ordinary Life

◆

Deborah Evans Hogan

Amethyst Light Ministry

Townsend, Massachusetts
2021

Published by Amethyst Light Ministry, Townsend, MA.

www.amethystlight.org

Cover photo gifted by Michelle Gold Mombrinie,
as well as photo on page preceding the title page.
Photos on pages 37, 67, 85, 87, and 163 by the author.

Edited by Kate Victory Hannisian
Blue Pencil Consulting, bluepencilconsulting.com

Book design and layout by Robin Wrighton
Wrighton Design, robin@robinwrighton.com

ISBN: 978-1-7371221-0-4

First Edition

Printed in the United States of America

• • •

*Dedicated to
Unconditional Love.*

• • •

Keep on praying for faith,
it is through prayer that you develop
all your wonderful qualities of soul.

~ Myrtle Fillmore

DEAR READER

Most names of clients and friends mentioned in this book have been changed for privacy. Please know, if you recognize yourself in my stories, and it feels different than you remember, that we each have our perceptions. Your experiences, these sharings, have the potential to help others see the world differently, to discover a life filled with their own extraordinary stories. Thank you for being part of my journey – in truth, we changed each other's lives, and now, hopefully, we will change the lives of others, too.

~ Deborah

TABLE OF CONTENTS

◆ ◆ ◆

Words are also seeds, and
when dropped into the invisible spiritual substance,
they grow and bring forth after their kind.

~ Charles Fillmore

◆ ◆ ◆

AUTHOR'S PREFACE

This book was not birthed to convince anyone of anything. We each have our individual views on life, and this is mine. This is an invitation for you to consider seeing life differently, living multidimensionally, and realizing that extraordinary possibilities are available to you. This book is an invitation for you to change the beliefs that construct your own stories, and watch your life change as a result. The combination of my insight and faith that I am sharing may be different than yours. I grasp that what is natural and easy for me is not so for everyone. I get that. Yet, I do believe it is *possible* for you to also have remarkable experiences that cannot be explained by linear logic. *I believe when we are ready, we each can partner with the mystical.* This is exactly why I share as I do and have done for nearly thirty years.

I offer this book, filled with what I see as exceptional Mystical moments, with the intention that other souls who have experienced comparable happenings will know they are not alone, nor are they crazy, delusional or "weird" (my clients' favorite term to cover an array of varied occurrences). I wrote this book to support your awakening awareness as a child of the Universe, a speck of Divine essence. I share these experiences to encourage you to apply your highest, most positive expectations of this amazing life, to fully know what are called miracles. How many of us welcome miracles as part of our everyday existence? Do you expect miracles in your life? Do you genuinely believe in them? Here is my secret: *I depend on them.*

I want transformation to be a grounded choice, not one far off in make-believe land. I want to take the idea of something that has been historically outside the realm of possibility for too many, to be seen as a natural option, at your fingertips. I want you to know, in order to have exceptional experiences, you only need to shift your attitude. I want you to see, that shifting your perceptions can be food for your soul, and nourishment for your heart.

There was a time when I did not depend on God. Perhaps you do not right now. Growing up, this was not shown in our family. No one I knew lived that way. Faith was not part of our household, either the word or the action. But I was given other openings to see, as I share with you in this book.

There was a time when I did not have the slightest conscious awareness about life. I was sheltered as a child. Sent away to overnight camp at nine, to Europe for the summer at thirteen, and to boarding school at fourteen. I can say that my upbringing was not one of inclusiveness. Family vacations were not a regular event. As a teenager, I did mindless, stupid things. I was angry with my parents, no doubt I was unkind to them at times, and my story is that I failed to live up to their expectations of me. I was always a loner, not a joiner. I did not fit the mold my family expected, nor any other. I felt unwanted in the family tribe, yet at the same time, something within me was okay with being me. In other words, being an outcast did not break me.

I do not have a story of being an alcoholic or drug addict, or of finding Jesus when I got sober. I do not have that kind of path to share. I have had many emotional ups and downs in my personal life. To others, I may have appeared to be an airhead with not much between the ears. At a near-fortieth reunion, a friend from high school told me I always appeared to be in a bubble. Other people would see restlessness and I saw experiences. Yet somehow, someway, things always worked out for me, and I always felt capable, whatever the issue was. During my entire life, I have sensed and seen beyond what was appearing in the physical. And now, I find myself here, in this place of sharing and hopefully influencing others for good.

Spiritual evolution is messy. It is not neat. Hence, these stories are not presented in the perfect order that I experienced them. I chose to categorize them to make a themed impact, rather than organize them by date—as if I even could! More often than not, until we have a palpable, personal and positive relationship with Spirit, we feel tossed around on a stormy ocean like a small boat with no anchor. Yet, when we find our anchor, when we finally realize what we stand upon, we can discover peace, acceptance, and extraordinary experiences in the midst of our everyday existence.

Do you wish to be in partnership with the mystical Divinity of life? Do you want to look to and trust Spirit? Do you want changes in your life—and are you willing to change your stories so they can be so? **Partnering with the mystical is about what you choose: what you choose to look at, choose to believe, and what you choose to have faith in.**

Three years ago, during a planning meeting with a few chosen Beloveds of my ministry for an upcoming public event, a young man named Jon turned to me. In the most nonchalant voice, he stated, "You know, Deb, you really should write a book about all your experiences." I instantly realized my experiences *were my story.* This suggestion had nothing to do with what we were discussing at the meeting. It was spoken as if it came from nowhere, but nothing comes from nowhere. Time has passed, and his words remain in me; an inspired directive. This young man is a writer himself. He mimicked what every psychic, intuitive, and healer had ever said to me, but for some Divine reason, that time, with the message delivered in his fully nonjudgmental, casual, matter-of-fact way, the book idea landed. From my heart, thank you, Jon.

Deborah Evans Hogan
July 2021, Townsend, Massachusetts

◆ ◆ ◆

The psychotic drowns in the same waters
in which the mystic swims with delight.

~ Joseph Campbell

◆ ◆ ◆

INTRODUCTION

———————

Being aware of mystical experiences will change your stories. Changing your story changes your experience. Changing your experience changes your life. Do you wish to heal relationships? To show up in the world differently than you are? Do you want to believe in goodness? To see your faith manifested in your day-to-day reality? Do you want your faith to expand to such a degree that you feel joy every single day? Do you pray to not be angry at the world, yourself, or others? Are you tired of the same old painful stories playing in your life over and over again—and never changing? Do you want to believe there is more to life than this three-dimensional reality? *Then you must stretch your concepts of life and in doing so, your stories will change. This book can help you do that.*

My goal with this book is to inspire you to notice effects (answered prayer, miracles) in your life due to you developing faith in the nonphysical. This nonphysical-ness, our Divinity, is a sacred well; it is where we can go for guidance. If the stories in this book resonate with you, perhaps you will remember and feel the eternalness of life, the expansiveness of all which we are part of. I wish for you to see and feel the evidence of a power greater than your human self alone.

Many people have limiting beliefs about life. We hold ourselves in restrictions, according to what we see before us. When we step outside the realm of linear boundaries and feel the multidimensional-ness of life, our stories change. Our stories, our experiences, what we create in our now, and what we carry as our lineage, all of this shifts. As we release our chosen restrictions attached to our perceptions, we are set free. *You have my promise: change your story and your life changes.*

The mystical is the Holiness of life which connects it all as one whole, yet goes beyond human comprehension. The mystical, that which we do not see directly but can feel, joins all life in a magnificent web. There are hundreds of names for It; God, Creator, Universal Intelligence, the Divine, the Great Mystery, and Divine Consciousness are but a few. The stories in this book are my evidence of a Higher Power, a nonphysical Presence, through my relationship with the Mystical. I fully believe that what you call It, whatever your name is for the Divine, is not important—but what we believe about It, and *how this helps us expand into a more open, loving, and joy-filled awareness, is important.*

What I know to be true about this earth journey is we are not here to "achieve" Divine perfection, for we are already that. Did you know you are Divine? Our Inner Being, our Higher Self, our True Identity, our Spirit is comprised of the innate perfection of Divinity. We come to earth to have tangible, emotional experiences not available to us anywhere else in the Universe. I have visited home (the other side/heaven) on two occasions I am aware of. It is luminous. This is the only word that truly fits. The colors of whites, silvers, pinks, and golds are filled with light themselves. Also, the Light! I found myself in the midst of radiant brightness, clearness, joy, and a profound, wondrous glow. There are "areas," but no buildings as earthlings think of them. There is no vegetation or ground. At home, there is *only* a vibration of unconditional love. Home *is* a vibration of unconditional love. The energy is pure love, *minus any human/ego emotional attachment.* In other words, there is no personalization. We can meet our earth enemy and take joy in an embrace, for we know there is only The Presence of the Divine. There is no frequency of fear, lack, right or wrong. There is no judgment, no malice, shame, or guilt. There is life and yes, there is learning. Interestingly so, a difficult concept to grasp from a human perspective—*we maintain an individual personality, minus the facet of human emotional attachment.* Perhaps the snowflake description works here; no two of us are alike, but we are each perfect, and a lovely speck of the Divine.

I depend on God for everything, the God of you and the God of me. I believe God is pure consciousness, the Creator energy that designed and gave birth to this universe. We can even think of God as our cosmic parent. I believe we do not see God, but we do see the effects of our faith in God and our application of that faith. God's designs and laws are always accessible to us, but it is our choice to consciously apply them, hence putting them into positive action. In my deeply personal relationship with Spirit, this beaming vibration of creative radiance is my absolute unwavering foundation. I call myself back to It each morning in my silent sitting and many times during the day as I find myself at crossroads. By sharing these intimate stories, I hope you will see examples of my many moments of choice, of opportunities to call upon God and to allow the Holy Spirit to lead me. In other words, opportunities for *me to get out of the way* and allow God's grace to transform a situation. Fearful thinking prevents us from hearing Divine guidance. **Understand, it is not that Spirit isn't (t)here, it is that we must stop, and be quiet enough to hear.**

When I refer to "knowing," when I use the term "I know," I am saying that the Universe, God, my Angels, Spirit Guides, or my Higher Self have nudged me, kicked me in the butt, pointed me in the best direction, or have downloaded information through undeniable nonverbal communication, telepathic juju, or intuitive feelings that I would never, ever choose to deny. Knowing is the feeling of certainty. *Knowing is what I believe in, and what I have proven to myself over and over again.* Through my journey of developing a *personal, positive, and palpable relationship with God,* I tried to ignore it, this certainty, and it always came back to me as a feeling of remorse. I wish I had, I should have, why didn't I? Now, I have grown to trust it completely.

As a spiritual counselor, I often hold space for pain and discomfort. I hear stories that could break a heart right open, even dampen hope, if I did not have faith in our Creator having created us with an innate ability to change, heal, mend, and find. In our desire and surrender to see differently than we already do, we can witness Divine Providence in our lives. We can search, seek and see the good, the blessing, and the love in any situation. I call this natural. Nothing is outside of God, for this is impossible. The Creator is in all things, each place, all of time and space, waiting to be revealed. The Divine is here, waiting for us to apply our faith to see It work in our lives. We are part of It and It is part of us. This is life: *An eternal string of moments in which it is our path, our joy, our nature, to recognize God.*

I have experienced enormous blessings in my life, blessings that offer grace and love in ways that are deep, tender, and unexpected. You can, too. I look back over my trials and see how I grew through them, how they helped me to seek different answers, solutions, and perceptions that I never even thought of as possible. I hope that you will have these experiences also, or at least be enticed to consider "other" when reading these stories. In the moments of challenges, which is us bumping up against ourselves, we learn more about ourselves, and I, for my part, learned much more about God. There are times in my life when listening to God, following Spirit's directives, has gone against another person's ego, rubbed them the wrong way. These moments can cause chaos, tears, distress, and messiness; divinely so, *creating the potential for change.* It is not always easy to let go of the old (we can be so good at hanging onto it!) to welcome the new. But, when done through faith, it can be a journey of excitement, security, and ease.

Taking action according to our inner guidance may mean leaving jobs for what appears to be non-sensible reasons, or ending relationships or even marriages, moving to where you know no one; yet, God has directed you, you were called, and you went. In other words, you are not *running from* in fear or sadness, but being *led to* by faith, through Holy instinct. In taking your choices personally, family and friends may feel forgotten, even though your action has nothing at all to do with them, and everything to do with trusting the language of Spirit, your intuition. In spiritual immaturity, someone may take other people's choices, actions, and words personally, as if another person's choices have to do with themselves.

When I talk about consciously following our inner God compass, I am referring to those who are doing or have done their emotional excavation, their spiritual heart work, who hopefully have a devotional practice, a practice of deepening their interior awareness and their belief in a Higher Power which is good. At this point, many can hear the difference between love or fear speaking, between their ego and Spirit. If you do not yet trust your communion with the non-physical, please find a teacher or a guide to support your path.

Going to church on Sunday used to be the way people believed they were fulfilling a spiritual calling. But for those who wish to fully embody an expression of what they know they are created from, Sundays alone are not enough. Remember, at Home (the other side), we are ALWAYS in it, eternally part of it, for that is ALL there is. Here on earth, there is a smorgasbord to choose from. Perhaps the faith of your family or what you grew up with no longer fits you. We must each create individual time to grow through spiritual practice, and to develop a palpable, positive, and personal relationship with Spirit through our inner caves and our heart centers.

As you read this book, my hope for you is that your perceptions, mind, and heart may open to the understanding that nothing is outside the realm of God, which extends into and through multiple dimensions. I hope that you feel inspired, encouraged, empowered, and willing to be transformed. There is not God... AND this or that. Everything is an effect of Creator energy, of the application of the Laws of God, of creative nature. When we learn this, we can consciously apply this to our individual lives. Each person was created of the Divine; every flower, tree, and bug is God's energy in form, awaiting our recognition for It to be enlivened.

Here I share evidence of the nonphysical, through words, ideas, and testaments which expose ways to see that our faith in Divine Intelligence, in this enormous, present, accessible, and eternal somethingness, is always here, *right where you are, wherever and whoever you are.* When you realize this, when you learn you can ask for help, you listen to the universe. The universe always responds, not because you are worthy, but because corresponding to your beliefs is a built-in mechanism designed by the Creator. Remember, faith is not something you go to the store and buy, or act a certain way and acquire. Growing faith is an experiential journey of listening to your inner guidance, trusting your gut, and surrendering to more. My faith in God took my commitment to self and devotion to the Divine. *Faith is developing trust in your inner knowing.* Faith is recognizing the innate intuition that sometimes gnaws at your belly, keeps repeating the same thing in your head, or makes your heart flutter, palms sweat and might even give you a joy orgasm just thinking about a yet-unforeseen idea; but always, in its silence, it is the loudest thing we have ever heard.

It is a simple truth, that we each get to where we want to be in our own perfect time. I ask you, is it your time now?

PART I

• • •

GROUNDWORK

• • •

The things that have been most valuable to me
I did not learn in school.

~ Will Smith

♦ ♦ ♦

When you behold the entire universe
as a play of consciousness
what is there to do but smile?

~ Amma

♦ ♦ ♦

1

PARTNERING WITH THE MYSTICAL

*Moments of mystical insight are difficult enough for
the recipient to understand, let alone explain to others.*

~ Alexander McCall Smith

◆

Making friends with the mystical aspects of life will change the way you live. In our human beingness, we do not see with our eyes what is called mystical, Divine, or heavenly. Yet, when your thinking shifts from a physical, concrete model to a more open model of believing in what we cannot yet see plus having faith that *your pure belief in its existence is enough,* you *will* see the effects of your faith every day. You will call these miracles, and eventually, you will come to expect more of them, *having risen from hopeful faith to faith-filled knowing.* This is partnering with the mystical. No one can teach you this; you have to show it to yourself.

What is the mystical? The Merriam Webster dictionary defines *mystical* as "involving or having the nature of an individual's direct subjective communion with God or ultimate reality. Ex: the mystical experience of the Inner Light." Other definitions refer to "mysterious circumstances" and "the supernatural." These explanations make partnering with the mystical sound unattainable. I disagree.

It is possible to live a life expecting your prayers to be answered, guidance to come to you, and Jesus, angels, and others to help you. You can live a life where you expect your faith to bring positive results, where you can see your word created in form and you can feel palpable knowing within your body.

Partnering with the mystical looks like God is our go-to. We pray first before we take another step. We discern first, before making a choice. We may begin and end each day in gratitude for what the Universe has presented through us. To partner with the mystical, to hear spirit-driven guidance, we must be willing to *surrender* (not the ego's favorite word), to know that we do not have all the answers, but we know someone or something does. We partner with the mystical by realizing that life is a co-creative effort, and that we must open our hearts in faith to the power greater than ourselves, to gracefully receive.

Each person has their unique journey. We are alone, yet collectively we are on an awakening exploration, a wandering from the head to the heart, to remember our innate beingness, our Divinity, our God spark. Have we forgotten or do we simply fail to remember? In that beautiful moment when we remember to see that there is another way of being, that miraculous experiences *can* and *do* happen in daily life, *everything changes.* I believe these encounters that many refer to as phenomenal (psychic, mediumship, healing, answered prayer, etc.) are the natural way. There is so much more to us, of us, and part of us than most people are taught to believe.

Each moment that we awaken to a deeper and deeper awareness of our soul aspect, what I call our True Identity, more joy is made alive in ourselves and on this earth plane. This way of living—intuitive, seeing, knowing, trusting—is the natural, innate way, and nothing else feels good to us. Think of feeling sad, depressed, anxious, wrong, stressed, fearful; none of this feels good, yet many people fully accept, without question, that this is the way life is. Why? Our human conditioning causes us to forget Divine existence and believe only in a linear, finite world— in other words, only what is tangibly in front of us. Many of us know we are miserable when we do not follow our instincts, our gut, our inner voice. Too often we ignore our gut because it may make another person feel bad or wrong, or we fear looking like a failure, or for the simplest reason: an authority figure or loved one does not agree with us. We ignore our happiness, joy, and callings to receive outside validation from others. Too often we ignore the "red flags" because we have been told what being polite is, or how life should look, or how we should be, or act, and especially, *what to believe.*

If our story is believing our humanness is separated (by some sort of tangible wall) from our Divinity, then we allow fears to squash our insight to see beyond what is in front of us. Due to many traditional religious and social conditionings, we play small. We are told we can never attain this or that. We are taught we are "less than" and will never be good enough. In needing to feel safe, people cling to what they see as concrete, which is finite, believing *that* is all that exists or all that is *real*. What many choose to believe in is only what they physically can see, to create a feeling of security—*which is a false sense of safety and never dependable.*

Why? Because what we see before us is always going to change. Is that not what history itself is? Humans change. Day to day and often moment to moment, based on emotions. The weather changes, as do the landscapes, housing, careers, jobs, and relationships. Everything outside of us is always changing. This is natural. We are continually shifting. Depending on something that naturally changes through its innate cycles called life may not be wrong, but it is sure to be disappointing. What is inside of us, what we are made of, created from, what we are part of *does not change.* This part of us is not tangible, not three-dimensional. We cannot see it. Our faith in this great stabilizer, a higher power, our belief in this unchanging somethingness; which is our True Identity, is how miracles occur in our lives. This, we can depend on, and should.

This earth journey is a most precious gift. It is my understanding that here is the only place in the universe where we experience duality and polarity, dire opposites of what we see as negative/positive and good/bad, thereby offering the earth soul journeyer wider choice and greater individual creative options. I can often be heard saying, "life is a banquet table, the dark at one end, the light at another; we get to choose what we take from the smorgasbord." We have a choice when we encounter fearful thoughts, to believe them or not, to engage with them or not, to feed them or not; for we have been created with **free will.** Fear will tell us to be afraid, that whatever our hope is, it is not possible, or that we cannot accomplish our dreams. Fear will do all it can to prevent us from delving deep into our heart center and *knowing* God. Why? Because when we do this, fear ceases to be. How? Because the Creator designed it that way. Take attention away from what you do not want and place it on what you *do* want. Attention = growth.

Fearful thinking creates a dark rabbit hole. It can call us in deeper and deeper as it builds momentum, *attracting more like itself.* In stopping right then and there when you have a fearful or negative (hopeless, resistant, shameful, angry, jealous, unloving) thought in your mind and take a breath, a pause, you create a space to choose a different thought and/or ask for Divine support. In choosing a positive, loving thought, you have flipped the switch to hear Holy Spirit guidance. (Sometimes we hear, sometimes we feel, and sometimes the response is simply an urge.)

As an ordained interfaith minister, I see the Christian cross as a symbol for our everyday moments of choice. Right or left? Up or down? Yes or no? Believe it or not? Agree or argue? Quiet or speak? Engage with that, or this? Each person, no matter one's physical age, encounters crossroads hundreds of times in one day. In every aspect of life, I try to remember to choose God. What do I mean? I mean I choose faith in goodness. I mean I choose tolerance, kindness, joy, health, forgiveness, potential, open-mindedness, laughter, love, and loving. When I am stuck, this offers me an opportunity to choose to believe there has to be another way, another answer I have yet to see, no matter the question. I choose to trust a Higher Power, the Divine Intelligence of the Universe, the mysterious Creator, the Source of all life; this is always my mindful goal. Do I ever fall short? Absolutely. In that humble awareness, I choose again. I am, as we each are, a work in progress.

Infinite Intelligence shines when we stand firm during a challenge, believing God is good all the time and that a nameless Higher Power exists. This is partnering with the mystical; we cannot see it, but we believe in it and then witness the effects of it in our lives. One of my stories is, *I partner with the mystical through acts of faith to co-create exceptional experiences for myself and my clients.* It is in the daily challenges that we are given opportunities to grow our faith, to raise our realization of the Divine, to exceed our previous level of trust, and climb higher than we ever dreamed possible. In believing in the Divine, partnering with the mystical, having faith in what you call God, and changing your stories, your entire life, every single aspect of it, changes. It is not only possible but natural to welcome exceptional blessings.

I believe we came here, to Earth, to humanhood, to this experience, to consciously choose the Divine out of other choices, to exponentially enliven the Divinity on this earth plane. This is the awakening journey, a path from the head to the heart, from thinking to feeling. Seeking choices from the perspective of our True Identity, we are happy to do so, for it is fun to recognize the Divine. No matter where we find ourselves, when we pause and go within, our awareness can then open to a palpably undeniable, nonphysical sacred essence of the Holiness of life.

In this awakening process, our sensitivities are heightened. Those who are empaths, mediums, and/or psychics can have a challenging time in public. Crowds, loud places, theaters, most television shows, anger, harsh language, unkindness, and ego all present resistance to an open, loving vibration. Most of us cannot retreat to a cave, and some do not want to. Many, like myself, believe we must be present in (some consciously chosen) social aspect of life, to *grow our spiritual core,* build it up to always have our faith first no matter how earth life looks, or what challenge/opportunity may exist. Yes, faith in action takes practice. Let's call these spiritual calisthenics. Exercising our faith!

The spiritual concept of being in the world but not of it calls those who walk a path of unconditional love to consistently recognize the spiritual God substance of their inner being *as well as everyone else's.* This takes daily renewal through a commitment to one's spiritual practice, which may or may not consist of meditation, prayer, reading, yoga, music, journaling, walks in nature, or listening to spiritual teachers in person or on the internet. It is a devotional re-filling of the well, realigning with Truth, so we do not fail to remember the great love we wish to be and express in this life.

Remember, as we can so easily forget that this earth journey is *meant* to be fun. We *can* LOVE the act of placing our faith first, of expressing our faith, being our faith, and living our faith. As we change our perceptions and our stories, our frequency heightens through remembering God, and we open to more than this three-dimensional existence offers; we open to Divine inspiration. In this, we are transformed and experience more joy than we knew was possible.

2

CHANGING YOUR STORY

Every choice you make has an end result.

~ Zig Ziglar

◆

Every single person is in partnership with *something*. What you are in partnership with is what you value most, what you give most of your time, attention and energy to, and what you give the most airtime to. Too often a woe-is-me story is played over and over again, as if that helps you to move forward, or will get you to a different place, or help you to see it differently. Ask yourself; am I in partnership with fear or trust? Am I in partnership with old stories? With illness? With doubt? Am I in partnership with health, loving, kindness? Am I in partnership with complaining, shame, or guilt? Am I in alignment with what if, what was, or cannot be? Do I value control, fixing, one way of acting, or forcefulness? Or do I value diversity, creativity, spontaneity, and fun?

Why is changing your story so relevant? Because how we perceive our experiences, how we carry our perceptions around with us in our energy field, creates an energetic well of emotions, *and this is the space from which we respond or react to life.* Every conversation, every experience, every moment we have is either responded to or reacted to, based on the stories that are held in our emotional grid. Any energetic/emotional attachment to our stories becomes our jumping-off point when we feel challenged, insecure and unstable; no matter how old the story, or how old we are.

Until we practice choosing to see from unconditional love, which for most people IS the spiritual path—to love as God loves us—we will remain in shame, guilt, and regret.

The ego causes us to believe that everything that happens in our life is about how other people are, not about how we are. Because this is how the ego/headspace sees, it causes us to be a victim and to lack empathy. The ego deplores true connection and thrives on the negative. There is a drastic energy difference between these two statements:

- My mother was an alcoholic and her addictive behavior messed up my childhood, and I am still blaming her for my bad behavior and my addictions.

or

- Eliese was an unhappy person who had little self-esteem and never spoke up. The only choice she saw was to stifle her pain with alcohol.

The first story makes us a victim, the second creates empathy for another human being. One story attaches us to a person's self-destructive choices, the other sets us free. One story will be a trigger for us for our entire lives, the other will not. **You can rewrite the story.** I promise you. You cannot change what happened, but you CAN change how you perceive any experience. Empathy will change your story. Empathy opens us to compassion. We see another's personhood and we forgive them their humanness. Empathy connects us in the very best way possible, which ironically, disconnects us from taking responsibility for another person's actions or responses. This is what it means to heal our stories. We rewrite them, speak them aloud, journal them, to not only see them differently but to carry them differently as well.

Forgiving does not mean accepting or agreeing. All our stories that are too heavy to carry and that are built of discordant attachment can weigh us down. When we have opened our hearts in recognizing everyone is here doing the best they believe they can do on this earth journey, we open a door to forgiveness. Meaning, *I will no longer carry your story as my own.*

What exactly opens the door to the likelihood of your mystical awareness? Yes, prayer. Also, a good ole' cry, or getting angry, or falling to our knees in exhaustion. Maybe a simple conversation, a glance, a moment with a stranger, laughing till we cry, any instance can ignite the feeling of the Divine. Each breath holds the potential for us, our hot-mess selves, to open to our inner being, our True Identity—to see another way, a different answer, a moment of immeasurable awareness. How exciting is that?

In all the studying and reading we can do, nothing is made "real" for us until we try it first, and prove it in our own lives, *for ourselves,* without a doubt. Willingness is required—the willingness to surrender, and allow another way to show itself. One of my first spiritual crossroads was reading about the Mirror Law – that I could not draw anything to me that was not already within me. Everything was and is a reflection. This is logical to me. Since we are pure energy, we reside at the center of our universe, of our movie, and all we bring to ourselves is a reflection of our energy grid. *Humans have been given free will to connect with a story, with others, with life, through either fear OR love.* I first implemented the Mirror Law when I would feel my buttons pushed. It was quite amazing. When another person got under my skin, and my old fear-based reaction would rise to the surface, I would stop, take a breath, and pause. I realized they were only showing me something that was within me. I would silently thank them, bless them and *go do my own work.* I would take responsibility for my choices, behavior, and the reflection before me. I would go change my story, go realign with a higher vibration, a more loving way of being. The question on this awakening journey is, are you willing to do your own work so you can see a more grace-filled and positive life for yourself?

3

TO ◆ BY ◆ THROUGH ◆ AS

Everyone is ripening at their own speed.

~ Mooji

◆

I t is humbling, caring, and wise to walk with this Truth: *everyone is on the same journey, and we are each in a different place on this path of awareness and recognition of our Divinity.* Why? Because we each have different perceptions, personalities, experiences, upbringings, and stories. "To, By, Through, As" is a loving and empowering awareness of understanding Universal Law. The above quote from Mooji succinctly expresses Divine patience, awareness, and love, all in seven simple words.

I have no idea who originally created the teaching To, By, Through, As, or who first wrote about it. I do remember hearing this teaching from a minister one Sunday morning in a Unity church. It has stayed with me as a compass to guide me to not judge, but to embrace all paths, to know we are each doing the best we think we can do, to be patient with others and myself, and to embody empathy rather than criticism. This extraordinary explanation, based purely on the energetic radiance of an individual, has also served me as a counselor and healer in recognizing and respecting where another person is "at" on their path. Our spiritual paths, our awakenings, are an inner journey. What we see outside of us, what we experience, is a reflection of our inner vibration.

Since it has been many years since I originally heard this teaching of To, By, Through, As, I have no doubt woven my own awareness within each of the four stages. Here I offer to you what I feel is a beautiful description of our "general" journey to know God. Many of us are in the gray area between stages, one foot in one, one foot in the other, making our way to the next stage. Is this not natural, reflecting our innate nature as we grow, age, develop and mature? Many times, no matter where you may see yourself predominately "at," we can each experience other stages, ever so slightly during a single day. To me, this offering may very well be the most linear explanation I believe can be offered of a Divine maturity process. The recognition of these stages can promote understanding, and perhaps even forgiveness, patience, and tolerance of ourselves and others. Please remember, there is no black and white here, no right or wrong, no good or bad, no better or worse. We are, where we are. And it is always a little of this and little of that.

TO

We seem to all begin here. Life is done TO us. This is a victim mentality of perceiving life. Life is done TO us, all happens outside of us, nothing is our fault, there is no comprehension of responsibility, we have no voice, no say, not one iota of the concept of empowerment. The common language is phrases like: "them, to me, they did this, I don't know, not my fault." When an adult is emotionally stuck in the TO stage, they are still blaming their parents for their life challenges. In other words, they have not yet realized they a choice—to stop playing the victim by changing their perception of their story. They were neither taught nor exampled choice. They are ruled (and well taught) by emotions. They are palpably reactionary. There is name-calling during this stage, expressing blame and shame.

A victim mentality has heavy energy, an unwanted vibration. A victim mindset holds firmly from conditioned roots of childhood from authority figures who did not yet realize the Divine themselves. In the TO stage, there is an obvious unawareness of unconditional love. The ego is running the show, so much so that a person may appear as broken (drawing compassion from others) and portraying the illusion of having no healthy ego at all. (In energy medicine, EGO stands for *Edging God Out,* and has polarity as well—too much and too little—with both unaware of a Higher Power.) There is no concept of a higher power, no interest in the spiritual life, no sense of nonphysical levels of existence. A person is very self-involved at this stage. This is what some may refer to as a three-dimensional mentality—and a wounded one at that. In this explanation, "wounded" means they are underdeveloped, not yet with any concept of their own, or anyone else's innate Divinity.

BY

At this stage, you are beginning to open to the dark side of EGO, and yet it is still energetically healthier than the previous level of TO, for you have shifted from outside self as a victim to an interior mode of being overtly responsible. (We could even see these first two steps as opposite; eventually, balance comes into play.) The BY stage is where the individual believes they are *fully* and *only* responsible for what they accomplish. I did this, I did that—I, I, I, me, me, me. This is all ego/mind. People in this stage are still without any acknowledgment of a Higher Power, of being part of a whole, of Divine connection. Humbleness is rare. This stage can be extremely defiant, with individuals not wanting any outside support, not looking at any other ways, perceptions, or opportunities, and not listening to ideas or recognizing their innate birthright. Everything is personal. Also, as this stage softens (as they each do, merging into the next), a sense of appreciation for certain aspects of life, usually of nature, comes to light.

THROUGH

"God is working THROUGH me" is the dominant realization of this stage. Prayer begins to enter, the idea of connection to "a power greater than I" has birthed. Here you are beginning to partner with the mystical. On the spiritual path, many people stay in this space for lifetimes. This is the time where people take workshops, classes, schooling, and their bookshelves are overflowing. The ego can be very full of itself, as a person still sees themselves as separate, as only a human body, as an individual, as a vessel that God can use as an instrument. At this stage there is less reacting emotionally. We begin to practice conscious *choice*. Unconditional love is brought into the mindset. Taking other people's speech personally happens less and less. Typical examples of language included: "this is done through me, God is working through me, healing happens through me, this instrument, this container, this body." People can speak of being extremely blessed at this stage as if others are not. Awareness of Oneness is not yet fully realized.

AS

In the full regalia of this AS awareness, we are in recognition that we are created of God's energy, made in Its image and likeness, and we are awake to our innate Divine connection as One—in spite of any human characteristics. Most of the ego has died or at least is no longer listened to. Fear does not exist here. All stories have been healed. Divine Consciousness is Sourced. No longer is there a frequency of you and I; there is only God. Devotion is the practice, the path. *To embody the radiance of AS is to merge into Oneness.* Any perceptions of personhood no longer exist. You are no longer responsible for anyone else's emotions, reactions, or choices. You love all. Grace is the flow. At this stage, when one is still in human form, joy is the way, faith is the nurturer, and love is the only answer. We live as the Holy Creators we are. You have experienced that Love is what allows, welcomes, and creates space for our awareness of God, as Divine Intelligence is Present. You know beyond a breath of doubt that surrender of the idea of "I" is a key to freedom.

Because we are each Divine Intelligence as a human form, I see us being able to have moments of AS—beautiful, incredible moments, as many spiritual teachers exemplify. Having moments of living as our True Identity, as a child of God, is not easy here on this earth plane; our human ego gets ruffled too easily. To *be* this fully, all the time, I doubt is possible until we leave our body and go home. Home is where *AS God exists,* there is only the vibration of unconditional love in that reality of what many call Heaven. I do see many teachers expressing this level of awareness, and I also know they live an earthly existence with aches, pains, and human interactions. When we are in a full embodiment of the Divine, we see by faith, not by sight. Here, we know the One Power of God, reaching out and through all life. Reaching this level of existence as "permanent" or as all there is to us, I do not see as an earthly opportunity. This earthly occasion is an opportunity to participate in tactile, diverse, palpable, and physical experiences in order to expand our joy, and in doing so, increase our personal awareness of God's unconditional love.

4

BEHIND MY FACE

Be yourself, everyone else is already taken.

~ Oscar Wilde

◆

believe the love of God is here for all of us, no one person more than another. I know Universal Law to be here for all. I want you, the you who is reading this right now, to know this, to have a sense of our ordinariness and our amazingness. It is very important to me that this book is not about me, **but about how faith in the Divine can bring you extraordinary experiences.** Yet, you need to know a bit about me first, before your full appreciation of these stories can blossom.

I am an ordinary person. My husband laughs hysterically at this statement. He repeats, "You are not like the other girls." This is true from his perspective. I may choose differently, but I am an ordinary human. (Which is quite extraordinary in and of itself.) I am not enlightened. I did not have a massive injury, or go to the Light down a long tunnel to death's door and turn back. I have not trekked the Himalayas or traveled to India to sit at the feet of a guru or meditated in seclusion for three years. As powerful as any one of these experiences would be and are for many, all I did and do daily is grow my faith and trust. In fact, for me, until this right-now moment, it was a very slow and gradual path, with many amazing aha moments, that in hindsight was traveled at a consistent and steady pace, for I was committed to proving God the good for myself.

People have called me gifted. I do not agree. Truth to be shared, I rather dislike the term. Saying someone is gifted implies they have something rare that others cannot have. Immediately this simple word takes one outside the group, separates a person from the crowd before they even enter the room. The human we see as "gifted" is simply someone doing what they love. We each have something we are better at than others, and we each have things we cannot do that others love to do. We each have things that come easily to us, and we each have things we struggle with. We are each part of the earth soup. We came here together and we are in it together.

I have come to realize I never walk alone. I believe the same for you. I believe this earth life is not the only life option there is in the universe. I believe and feel that there are ascended Beings with us. I have come to know there is more. I know there is always another way of seeing, an answer I have not yet thought of, an option not yet revealed. I know love is the great healer and that our choices are limitless.

I believe in our innate birthright as children of the Creator. I believe in extraordinary experiences. I believe everything is a miracle, for I believe all good is the Divine in form. I believe in the web of life, how everything is perfectly connected, how when we are not afraid to look, it all makes sense. I continually see this web, with dots as all the people I know, and how we each intersect, somewhere.

I do not believe in coincidence. The word "coincidence" is for people who do not yet understand Universal Law: *where we place our attention grows.* Every person is consistently creating through their word, vibration, and beliefs. As you may have read many times, we create either consciously through knowing or unconsciously through a state of not-yet-aware. We cannot help it; we are children of The Creator and therefore we are always creating.

I know we are part of something magnificent. I know that if I thought I was here on this earth doing life by myself, I would feel fear too, as many people do. I observe people who are struggling because they think they have to find a way, they have to figure out the answer, that all this is up to them and their human self alone. I know people who cut themselves off from life because it feels too challenging. You know what? If I did not know God, I see how life would be challenging and frightening. If I believed I was all alone —that is, without the nonphysical awareness I have—I would no doubt feel fearful, tired, and anxious. I understand. I get it.

There is much love here for us. There are many positive Beings and energies aligned with Love, Light, and Truth, here to help, guide, and support. *We must be willing to surrender, to learn and practice Universal Laws so we can embody the miracle-mindedness of life, to know of Divine possibilities.* I know this because I have lived it; I am living it.

I detest labels. Growing up in a home where labels were worshipped, I realized at an early age that their only purpose was to divide, never to unite. I have been called an empath, healer, intuitive, artist, channeler, transition doula, minister, shaman, weird, clairvoyant, clairaudient, claircognizant, a medium, a Reiki Master, counselor, guru, teacher, an HSP (highly sensitive person), multi-dimensional, a master energy practitioner, psychic, and I imagine even other names after I have left the room. My blessings are also my curse.

I dislike the term "sensitive." And yet, I say it often to describe myself, for many times words fail a cosmic association. In our humanness, I feel people see being sensitive as a weakness, giving it a negative connotation. Once a loved one thought I must be very anxious, for they felt it went along with being sensitive. This is not true. Being open, being aware and attuned to the energy of people, things, and experiences is a blessing, for it makes me very good at my work—yet its nature means that I require equal downtime, rest, and renewal. Hermit-like is my nature, yet interacting with another who is open to my offerings is a necessary joy for me.

I believe all is for good and I refuse to dwell on the negative, gossip, or watch the news. Not much of a dinner party conversationalist! I know you before you know yourself; this is a curse for social interactions, and a blessing for my work as I guide you to discover your own stories. I simply do not see the world the way most people do. I see the energy of a situation, of an expression, not the linear experience with possibly blame and fault. I see what others are feeling. A niece once called me to ask a question, simply because I always have a different answer than everyone else. I especially remember the day a group attendee once said to me; "Deborah, you are not everyone's cup of tea." And this is why there are hundreds of teas to choose from!

I am in private practice as a trans-denominational minister, counselor, spiritual guide, and energy practitioner, with all of the previously mentioned labels perhaps being part of a session—or not. I am ordained through The Universal Brotherhood. My studies are nonreligious, focused on meta-physics and New Thought. I am not a theologian. In my view, God is pure creative energy, a powerful presence that designed the universe according to order. Although I have many statues and pictures of what one can call deities in our home, to me they are human beings who express an unwavering faith and devotion in the Divine, which goes by hundreds of names. In my thirties, I made a conscious choice to study holistic health, energy medicine, faith, spirituality, and esoteric teachings. It appears that each following decade I delved in a little deeper. Now, engaged in multiple disciplines, having explored with hundreds of clients as a healer and woman of faith, as well as having been in church ministry for nine years with Unity, Science of Mind, and a church I began, the Church of Spiritual Empowerment, I have proven to myself *that a vacancy is a cry for God. A vacancy becomes an opening when we un-cling from linear rigidness and allow the mystical to guide us.* I love that description.

Perhaps awakening is going from clinging to non-clinging, from rigid to flexible, from closed to open. I have grown to believe God is one-stop shopping for all my needs. Crazy, right? I understand, and I mean it. No matter what I want, I go there, to God. In reading this book, perhaps you become more willing to trust that which you cannot yet see, or your concept of "possibilities" will increase. Hopefully, your understanding of and faith in a Universal Creator will expand.

As of this writing, I have been on a conscious spiritual path for forty-seven years. An intentional awareness began when I was nineteen years of age during my first marriage, where a joyful communion was not found. Wedded in October, we were emotionally separated by December. Yet, like many of us, I stayed, for ten years. I stayed until it was unbearable and I was emotionally depleted. Not pleasant. My therapist at the time let me off the hook of self-blame. "Deborah, when you put your money in a bank and do not get any interest, you move it to another bank." It did not take long for me to realize I was not getting any interest back on my investment and that I was alone in that marriage, and to see our differences and both our inabilities to connect emotionally, and to feel more of a struggle than not. *I just had no idea what to do about it.*

Because we had polar opposite upbringings, communities, and values, I imagine he felt alone in the marriage also. I learned he was secretive and did not always tell the truth. I learned I had no voice of my own, only the beliefs of my parents. My husband and I had not lived together before the wedding; we had not even vacationed together. What was I thinking? Blindly in love, I did not think at all. I was following the family rules. I was being a naïve good girl. A very young good girl. In year two we bought a house, in year six I gave birth to our son. All the while, I never stated my unhappiness, discontent, or fears. I did an excellent job of pushing them down and ignoring them. I probably did not want to make him look bad, or feel like a failure myself. I had not been taught to express my feelings. I did such a good job of putting on a happy face that my own family had a hard time believing me when I finally did speak up. I consider this marriage, as challenging as it was, to have been a powerful contract of souls, which caused me to choose differently. I learned that as I chose different thoughts, my story changed. As my stories changed, so did my life.

When I left the marriage, my mother was appalled and attempted to have me institutionalized. My parents had my newly separated husband and our son to their Florida home to visit, not me. Through this experience, I learned I had a choice in all matters, as to how I was going to choose to perceive *any* situation. I learned about myself, or at least who I might want to be; someone stronger, wiser, and more substantial. It took me years, but I found I had a voice, opinions, and ideas. My "wasband" was emotionally abusive, as he was taught and conditioned to be as a child. He was an excellent teacher for me in that he prompted me to seek alignment with unconditional love through forgiveness. Our marriage jump-started me to look for different, for more. I appreciate the role he played in my journey of self-realization. Our relationship is part of what makes me who I am today. How can I not be grateful?

In the vacancy I felt in this marriage, I was directed into myself, seeking to make sense of the life I was experiencing. I soon realized that I had forgotten what I knew as a child. In contemplating memories of being a young girl, I remembered knowing of cosmic "other": what may be labeled paranormal, spiritual, intuitive, or mystical. It is common for children to see with clear sight, to see the magic in the world, to have invisible friends, to speak of angels, and to see the colors of people's vibrations. Yet, it is not as common for an adult to look back and remember. Have you seen these things? Can you remember?

As a child, my pure heart told me we had and could communicate with spirit. It was all very natural. I knew God was right here with me. I knew my childhood dreams had a sense of other reality. To me, Jesus was a real person as well as my friend and sometimes my playmate. I instinctively knew I could accomplish anything I put my heart and mind to. *This was not intellectual knowledge of the head, but a deeper realization of the heart, as it remains to this day.*

My childhood inner awareness of nonphysical support was challenged throughout my life by my mother. I could make, build, create anything I put my mind to. I sewed without patterns, I built wooden toys, I cooked without recipes. All of this was threatening to an insecure woman. My instincts were not recognized, rewarded, or encouraged. As you read on you will come to know my mother as my single greatest teacher, an enormous blessing in my life. I am deeply grateful, for I would not have developed into who I am without her. It is a very beautiful and forgiving inner heart experience to see those we have been victimized or challenged by as very possibly an unconditional loving gift intended for us to reach, grow and expand our consciousness.

Post-divorce, in my early thirties, I tended bar, one of many careers. I have this distinct memory of three male friends of the owner who sat at the bar several evenings a week. They were rude, callous, ungenteel, and uncouth; gossiped about women they had been with; and made ignorant jokes and inappropriate remarks. They were also financially successful local businessmen. I wondered why. How were they so successful? My small-mindedness thought: they were not well educated; they did not fit any of the criteria my WASP parents had guided me with (which at this point in my naïve life was all I had to go on). I was baffled as well as disillusioned. I remember asking myself, why them? They were not nice people. Then I saw it, in a flash: *they fully believed in themselves.* They thought very highly of themselves. They believed they could, so they did. This was one of those lightning bolt aha moments for me. They also helped me remember what I had failed to remember, what I knew as a child. *Belief got them to where they were.* I felt inspired to know more. I immediately thought, *how could this concept of belief benefit my life?*

I now understand how the power of belief works. I have learned that belief works as law. What we believe in, we get. What we believe in, we naturally pay attention to. What we think about, we are bringing into our awareness. What we talk about, read, or spend time with, *we are allowing into our energy field.* Universal Law means *this goes for everybody.* Some call it a Law of God or nature. *It is done to us, through us, and as us, according to our faith.* Our thoughts become our beliefs and these create our perceptions or lenses, how we see the world. I have listened to hundreds of stories, each one based on a person believing something, then seeing it witnessed in their lives. I have watched a client change their story, resulting in different and more positive outcomes in their lives. I have witnessed bodies heal, relationships change and individuals go from playing a victim to feeling empowered. My beliefs, my faith in the Divinity of our existence, has allowed me to change my own stories, ensuing new and improved experiences. I expect them.

In my first position on staff at a church, my mentor said to me, *"Deborah, you'd make a great minister if you only liked people."* Embedded in my memory, this comment came to me over twenty years ago. In hindsight, it was true, but at the time it was unbeknownst to me. It was kindly stated and meant to be helpful, although I certainly did not receive it that way. I am not sure what she saw, or how I was behaving, but I did trust and still do trust this mentor's perceptions. I was spiritually immature, probably coming from illusions of self-grandeur and ego. My persona was good, my interior lacking. As I look back, I see I was not standing upon any substance. I could talk the talk, but I was not in complete integrity of walking it as well. Fortunately, the founding minister of this church was wise enough to see this and faithful enough to tell me so. I still had years of evolving, of life, of experiences to come close to expressing as the person, woman, and minister I had yearned to be. I knew then, and still do, that I wanted to *inspire others to create a personal, palpable, and positive relationship with God.*

In my spiritually immature years, I thought people had found IT, whatever IT was, and *then* came to church to share IT. Hence, my exasperation with humans. I see now this was the most perfect reflection of myself. I thought I had IT too! What is IT? Perhaps strong faith, knowing God, an awareness of the Divine, and loving humanity? I had a long way to travel to adore, love, and recognize God in each person I met. I had a ways to go to see the good, to trust the process of realization, and to move from my intellect to my inner knowing. First, I had to *humbly* recognize God's Light in and as myself. I think I had a pretty high horse to get down from.

Spiritual growth, the path from our heads to our hearts, is ignited through all the pushing and pulling we rile up in one another. There's the blessing. People's perceptions of life inspire me—either way, whether I agree with them or not. Isn't it incredible that two people can look at the same situation and see it differently? I am an open book; anyone can ask me anything. Many may think being an open book is unsafe, so they choose to protect themselves. Some may see a difficult life, but the person living the life may be the happiest they have ever been. A friend thinks our home is big, yet I do not have enough room and want larger. Think of it—even colors look different to different people. My perception of a person's belief in smallness, in a lack of faith, in only one right way to be—I see these as openings. Others may call it anxiety, sadness, depression, illness; I see a vacancy, waiting to be filled with recognition of the mystical, the magic, and the Divine.

When a person can think that we are alone here, believing that we are the only beings in this infinite universe, I am stunned. (As I am sure my experiences sound like made-up science fiction to them.) When a person states that there is no God, no Divine otherness, or has no sense of the nonphysical aspects of life such as intuition and inner knowing, I feel my gentle fierceness fire up. *Every single person I meet moves me.* Either way they see life, whether through fear or through love, increases my faith. They add to my evolving growth as a woman of God, a teacher, and hopefully an awakening soul. Every single person we engage with can cause us to look deeper within ourselves *when we invoke the courage to go there.* We may see ourselves as small, almost nothingness, but then in a miracle moment of shifting our thinking, our entire life can change to an understanding of eternalness, to what I call "other," to an enormity of potential, to acknowledging the sacredness of this existence, to seeing miracles, magic, and delight. This just blows my mind. *One thought can change everything. How spectacular is that?*

When I was growing up my favorite shows on television were the faith healers practicing the laying of hands upon others for Divine intervention. The crutches dramatically tossed aside, the wheelchairs left in the front row as people got up and miraculously walked. I was all in. Mesmerized. Glued to the television set, I was starstruck. My mother would enter the room murmuring, "This is all fake, Debbie, shut it off, it is foolishness." I did not care. It was true for me; somewhere within me, this resonated. I soaked it up. I wanted more.

As is true for each of us, my upbringing has inspired me beyond what I believe my human mind can fathom. I chose through sacred contract the perfect family to incarnate with. My parents' materialistic mindset, my mother's alcoholism and her many surgeries and insecurities, my father's shallowness and lack of emotional intelligence all made it clear to me that neither of my parents was satisfied, healthy, or happy. There was an emotional disconnect inside each of them, a vacancy individually that attracted them as a couple.

In my childhood home, there was never mutual dialogue. There were spoken and unspoken rules. The limited conversation was focused on stating judgments, opinions, and biases. Other than behaving in a way that my parents saw as proper conduct, we had little communion. There was no depth of discussion, no critical inquiry into life, never a look into or interest in another way of being. Other than one painting of an ancestor's sailing ship, art did not adorn my childhood home. Many mirrors did. I remember no books, except the encyclopedia. Faith, God, choices, or human questions of motivation, drive, or incentive were never discussed. My parents demonstrated that how they lived would not work for me. Their choices were not producing positive results. Included in behaving as I was told was my weekly task to elbow (jab) my father when he loudly snored during the Sunday morning church service, embarrassing my mother. If I had known what being appalled was then, that would have been it.

We each carry the stories of our upbringing within our energetic framework, our emotional grid. In other words, anything we are attached to through love or fear becomes part of our grid. These attachments form our perceptions, the lens we see life through. This is part of our childhood (those formative years) conditioning. The emotional takeaway of each story has a vibration; perhaps it is a vibration of anger, resentment, shame, being loved, feeling safe, hurt, or of joy. Perhaps an adult with a history of childhood illness matures to work in the medical field; so, is the history of illness a negative memory, or a blessing someone can find a way to be grateful for? What if a child who grew up in a series of foster homes matures to become a successful therapist *because* of their history? Yes, we can see any experience as a blessing and a curse, but which do you put more value on? Which story do you tell more often? I choose to value the blessing part more. Due to how I carry the story of being brought up by shallow, disconnected parents, I am personally, consistently inspired by what I perceive as "vacancy": people who are unhappy, unfulfilled, addicted, fearful, sick, drunk, bored, unhealthy or defensive. To me, these symptoms are a vacuum to be filled, an alms bowl waiting to be lined with gold, a heart waiting to be touched with love.

As a child in the early sixties, under the age of ten, I would think to myself, as I listened to my father react to the television, why does the color of their skin matter? Why does who that person loves matter to you? I was inspired by my father's prejudices, for they made absolutely no sense to me. I asked myself: How does he think that way? It was clear to me at a very young age, colors and genders had nothing to do with loving. I was inspired by the depths of my mother's sadness, her discontent, and physical pain in conjunction with my father's inability to notice, to not be emotionally moved to express caring. All this left me deeply perplexed. Now, I realize that he could not see her pain because he had yet to see his own. His unconscious response was to ignore her emotions. He could not give what was not yet alive within himself. Vacancy. Inspiring to me.

I live to recognize the Divine in all of life. This means I fully recognize a Higher Power, that which is greater than I. My daily goal is to see Holiness in you and me, to fully believe in miracles and Divine intervention as the way life can be. I want to live each moment of my life in partnership with the mystical, not thinking of it as too high an ambition, as unattainable, but to see each of us, as children of God with *immense potential.* I believe we each can get there, if we choose, to live a life of unquestionable faith in what we cannot yet see as being possible.

To the dismay of the human intellect, there are no concrete directions. How can there be? Each person is unique, each life a different path. Faith takes building trust through small steps and surrendering to that which we cannot see. It takes practice. It took me years and years to hear the still small voice. Yet I promise, once you do, you cannot shut it off. If we are truly devoted, *may it become all we hear.*

I believe we all have the potential to discover an exceptional existence. I consider intuition to be an innate, natural birthright; a part of the Great Architect's original design. This does not mean I am not in awe each day of my life; I am. And yet, I am never surprised. Our being born is Divine intervention. A body comes out of another body? Really? Why stop there?

Perhaps twenty years ago or so, during a class on prayer, I was asked, "How come you get answers from God, how come you feel angels around you, how come you hear guidance and I do not?" My answer was and still is, "because I expect to." I consider myself a common person with an uncommon faith in God, in the Universe, in this life, and in what we are created from. My faith is in *That*—no matter what *It* is called.

◆ ◆ ◆

The mind of the spirit will guide you
in perfect ways,
even in the minute details of your life,
if you let it do so.

~ Charles Fillmore

◆ ◆ ◆

PART II

◆ ◆ ◆

EXTRAORDINARY EXPERIENCES
OF AN ORDINARY LIFE

◆ ◆ ◆

Every single person is on a spiritual journey. Many are unaware of this, making comments like, "That person is not spiritual." Others are awake to the fact that nothing and no one is outside of God. The creator made them too. We are each here to wake up to being loving. The word "love" carries a human understanding that you need to find (some with an urgency) someone to love and who loves you. Loving is to live from feeling and being love in action, no matter what or who is before you. We are each here to recognize the Divine. We have diverse paths and various callings, yet we all end up at the same place. We each have different perceptions and stories. Yay! Diversity! Now, I will share some of mine.

◆ ◆ ◆

You have to grow from the inside out.
No one can teach you,
No one can make you spiritual.
There is no other teacher, but your own soul.

~ Swami Vivekananda

◆ ◆ ◆

5

A COSMIC TWO-BY-FOUR UPSIDE MY HEAD

Sometimes good things fall apart
so better things can fall together.

~ Marilyn Monroe

•

"You have cervical dysplasia," my gynecologist said. "It is pre-cancerous now, but heading that way. I want to remove it. Okay?"

No, it was not okay with me. So, we made a deal. Even though I worked in mainstream nursing home management, I was beginning to choose alternative health care for any of my own physical ailments. I had read Shakti Gawain, all the Seth books, and carried Louise Hay's little blue book *(Heal Your Body)* with me like a bible. (I still have my original copy, torn, loved, and coverless.) I chose a chiropractor to treat my migraines after I had been hospitalized where a doctor who did not know me prescribed Valium. I was thirty-something at the time. I held the bottle in my hand and just so I could hear, I stated out loud, "No thank you." Chiropractic care had worked instead. My gynecologist, Jeanne, knew how I felt about anything invasive and knew about my path of holistic healthcare. She listened to me and my out-of-the-box ideas. We agreed on six months. I had to make an appointment six months from that day and if my choices had not worked, she would surgically remove the dysplasia or, as she directly stated to my face, I had to find a new doctor. Okay. Deal.

Even though I somehow (through God's Grace) had stumbled my way through many emotional obstacle courses before this diagnosis (as in divorce, emotional abuse, my upbringing, co-parenting), this word "cancer" sparked a universal fear-based place, as it does so naturally. This time, for me, this particular obstacle felt deeply personal. It was residing inside *my* body. Ultimately, I was in this by myself. I, and only I, had ownership of this. I was to make choices for myself. Up until this point in my journey, I do not think I had ever looked so deeply at my own stories.

Wake-up calls. We all have them, don't we? We have these spiritual two-by-fours that slap us on the head and scream, "This is up to you!" We have these moments when the light goes on: My happiness is up to me, it is up to me to get sober, to get out of an abusive cycle, to get a job, to stay in school. We have a moment of great clarity that it is up to us, and we can no longer blame anyone else or hold them accountable for our choices. We can no longer blame our parents, our bosses, our ex-spouses, or anything that happened to us as a child. We have these moments when it feels like all is against us when in Truth, God is SO for us, and we have this opportunity, this gift, to *now* make conscious choices. We get to discover what we are made of. We can no longer look outside ourselves for answers, for we finally see that doing so has never worked. We have no choice but to seek within. We become self-responsible. These are the blessings of a cosmic two-by-four.

And so, my own inner journey began. One week, I went to a masseuse who also practiced Reiki and the next week to get acupuncture—both for the first time in my life. Even though I exploded with joy after both first sessions, they left me with palpable, obvious, and questionable effects. As the Reiki practitioner held her hands above my physical body, I felt discomfort in my belly. How was this possible? After my first acupuncture treatment, I was awake all night with belly pain, watching the clock until an appropriate hour to call and ask for help. When I did reach the acupuncturist, she gently and without hesitation suggested I rub my belly in a circular motion in one direction, and if that did not feel better, try the other direction. She taught me the pain was a *positive* sign, for energy was moving. As we were on the phone, I followed these simple instructions; the pain stopped immediately. How could I ignore that something was happening here? I continued these biweekly appointments along with chiropractic care to have my spine as healthy as possible. I spent my lunchtime at a local health food store that carried books. I let my inner guidance lead me. I bought what felt right for me, from books to supplements. I ate better. I did forgiveness work regarding my childhood and my perceptions and beliefs about my parents. I revealed a strength I never knew I had, the knowledge I never knew existed and change that I never thought was possible.

I gained the following invaluable insight (in the form of a question) through this threat to my health: *How did I want to show up in this experience?* It is the same answer, no matter the experience, every time I ask this of myself: *faithful.* Faith in God, in my choices, in my gut instincts, in my word. Stepping into love from love and not giving fear the time of day; this is how I wished to show up then—and now.

To heal this invasion in my belly, I had to rewrite two major stories. One was about my mother, the other, about my father. Like so many people, I felt like and therefore lived as a victim of my mother's choices. I began by retelling her story in a detached manner, by stating, "a young girl named Eliese." Not saying "my mother" immediately redefined and humanized her. As I stood outside our relationship, I was able to come to empathy and to declare choices for myself that were unique to me and not hers.

For my father, I had to go deeper. I remember the day I went to my bedroom, closed the door, sat on my bed, and imagined an empty theater. I sat in the center of the audience seats. I pictured my father as he walked onto the stage, flooded in lights. As if he had been transported to my vision, he walked with a cane, was flustered, asking where he was and what was happening. I spoke. I told him I had invited him here to listen to me. He asked me, "Why?" I explained I had things to say to him, unspoken things. I asked him to sit. He responded as if he was physically there in person. I heard his voice. He could not see me because the theater's house lights were off. I was in the dark. I was in total control. This was MY story. I shared with him the moments embedded in my mind that were not appropriate to me. I shared what I saw as a lack of boundaries. (This story is not about physical sexual abuse, but about a blatant lack of boundaries.) I shared memories and statements that were held in my heart as uncomfortable. He was deeply sorry. He cried. I explained that I know he loves me, this was not about love. Both my parents did the very best they could do with what they had emotionally and who they were. This particular experience was about me finding my voice, and I thanked him for agreeing to join me. I knew our souls were communicating. I knew that healing was taking place. My belief was and is, we do not have to do forgiveness work in physical person, face-to-face.

It was quite amazing what came from this experience. The next time I saw my father was at his Florida home, shortly before he transitioned, as he sat in a wheelchair. I knelt next to his chair to see his face and say hello. After greetings, he said to me, "If only I was younger, I would be knocking on your door." I took a gentle breath and said, "You know, Daddy, that is impossible because you are my father." Talk about a cosmic two-by-four. At near forty years of age, I finally spoke my truth, calmly and lovingly, with no anger, regret, or blame—just fact.

After dinner, my mother brought him to his room. I went in to say goodnight. He asked me about death. He authentically shared he was afraid to die. This was the very FIRST and final authentic, deep, meaningful conversation my father and I ever had. The tool of a visionary healing moment transformed us both, through all of time and space, shifted our story, and changed who

I was in our relationship, and therefore in my life. I showed up as I always had wanted to. I had changed my story.

At any crossroads, a moment of making a decision, facing a challenge, or in anticipation of a difficult conversation, ask yourself, *how do you want to show up in this experience?* You may want to be brave, courageous, open to understanding, flexible, forgiving, inspired, nonjudgmental, confident, or humble. Too often, we focus on how the other person should show up. Whatever you feel so moved to be in the midst of any experience, let it be positive, let it make you feel good about yourself. Decide, ask and go forth!

My scheduled six-month gynecological checkup turned out to not happen until a year had passed. I had made the six-month appointment, but evidently, God had a different calendar. The checkup appointment, just on the six-month mark, I fully prepped for. Valerian drops and flower essences—taken. As I sat in the waiting room, my name was called from the business office. They had not received my physician's referral. I could not be seen without it. My memory is I was not pleased, perhaps even irate, for I blamed this on the doctor's office. I made a second appointment for a few weeks out. I called beforehand to double-check they had received the referral. My appointment was at a satellite office, and this was in the days before computers. They had the wrong patient file. Wrong manila folder. Really. Same name. Same birthday! Same primary care practice, but looking deeper, different physicians. More apologies. I was mad. So I thought, "Twice this has been messed up! Why can I not get this over with?"

During this healing journey of cervical dysplasia in my body, even with my spiritual and holistic focus, one day at work I verbally snapped at a nurse. Not my way. Rude. Out of character. Unkind. Unprofessional. My boss and I decided I needed a break. After apologizing to the nurse, I left work that day to take one week off. Setting my easel up in my loft, I painted. Every single day. The light in my new condo was perfect. I cranked music, and the colors flowed. As I gazed out the windows, one block back from the main street, I watched a "for rent" sign go up in the window of a beautiful old brick building. Right then, I called the number. I went to see it. I rented it. I would open an art gallery. I needed a place for all my paintings.

Honestly, it happened like that, without any linear thought about "how would I get artists?" Oh, they will come to me. Really, how did I know that? Had I ever run an art gallery? No. No business plan, no experience; just a gut calling.

A week later, when I went back to work, I gave my one month's notice. This spirit-led choice was the first time I lost a friend due to saying yes to my inner guidance. She was furious with me. She asked, how could I do anything so irresponsible? I answered: Because, up until this moment, nothing had ever felt so right, so easy and so good.

By the time I made it back to my gynecologist, or rather by the time the stars aligned, a year had passed and the gallery was open. My doctor's appointment was the first time I had taken time away from my new venture. When I walked into the office, Dr. Jeanne greeted me. It was midmorning. "Come on in, you're my last patient. I will explain," she said.

Jeanne went on to share that she and her family had gone on vacation out west, to Arizona. They loved it so much, she had bought into a new medical practice and was moving there. I was her final patient. We discussed the choices I had applied to my healing journey. She surprisingly stated that "things" looked good, but took a Pap smear anyway.

Three days later on my answering machine was her voice: "Debbie, this is Jeanne. Your Pap smear is clear. This is your first unquestionable Pap. I do not understand how you did it, but I hope to find out. Keep it up. Goodbye."

I believe God gave me the time that was needed for me to get my act together, discover more, and allow time for the dysplasia to heal. There were no mistakes made by the business office or having the wrong patient folder; everything was for my benefit. It was perfect.

gallerie #40 - Washington Street,
Haverhill, Massachusetts, circa 1993.

To date, this is my biggest kick-in-the-butt-cosmic two-by-four I have experienced. Up until this point, I had only read a lot of books. This was before I became ordained, or a Reiki Master, or studied anything metaphysical. I was reciting affirmations, but not going deeper. The dysplasia diagnosis happened before I opened my first healing center, gallerie #40. At the time, I was a hospice volunteer and worked as the in-house public relations director of a nursing home. I certainly had a sense of cosmic life, but it was not yet my passion. This experience launched me into an unknown, to where only my inner guidance could have taken me; and it certainly did.

My healing experience of cervical dysplasia was just the beginning of what may be called an awakening for me. This art gallery/healing center was a very special place that opened doors I never even knew existed or had dreamed of. People came from all over New England to the gallery and sat all day, talking and having coffee for hours. I was selling little art, but people loved the gallery vibe. I never had to seek out artists, they found me. Soon after my Reiki training I set up a table in the back room and began seeing clients. Other certifications followed. Healers came from near and far as if I had put out an SOS. I hosted meditation nights, classes, and workshops. I produced local health fairs, was asked to have my own local cable television show, and was a frequent radio guest.

The week before I opened the gallery, I had hung on my bedroom wall a huge sign that read: "LEAP AND THE NET WILL APPEAR." (John Burroughs). It was directly in front of me, the first and last thing I saw each day. As it has been said before about this quote, we must act as if, we must trust as if, we must go forth in faith to see desired results.

Looking back, it felt as if the tightly wound beingness of my spirit had been set free by opening this gallery/healing center. Who could have known that my impatience with a nurse would be a light switch for self-discovery? I had no preconceived ideas of what this art gallery would bring me, yet it did bring me healing my relationship with my parents, entering the healing arts, and studying metaphysics. Each was pivotal to who I am today.

6

PIVOTAL MOMENTS

Two roads diverged in a wood, and I—
I took the one less traveled by,
And that has made all the difference.

~ Robert Frost

♦

believe we choose our parents. On a spiritual level, this had intellectually made sense to me for years. Without any substantiated proof for myself, other than reading many books on this subject, I had no self-evidence. However, it was not until my alcoholic mother and I had our first authentic conversation that this truth was known to me. Until this point in our relationship, at which I was then forty years of age, I thought I had gotten the wrong parent. I was sure, in my next lifetime, I would have a real parent, a healthy mother, one who was not self-absorbed, one who would not ask her friend to take her own child to her first day of boarding school because she instead chose to play in a golf tournament. I dreamed of a mother who would not fall asleep in the early evening from too much scotch or require back rubs from her young daughter, or awake to begin her day with a cigarette while she hid her early-morning dose of courage in a kitchen cabinet. How I dreamed of a mother who would not get drunk at a friend's house, causing her car to fall into a ditch on the way home, giving her ten-year-old daughter a strong enough hit to the dashboard to produce a massive black eye, migraines, and the need for future chiropractic care. (This was at a time pre-safety belts in cars.) I wanted a mother who would remember my friends' names, who I did not have to repeat stories to again and again, who did not call me several times in one evening because her drunken mind failed to remember we had already spoken moments before.

In the early '90s, my mother had come north to New England from Florida to visit family. One day my brother dropped my mother off at the gallery so she could see firsthand my new venture. Within its first six months, my art gallery had evolved into a healing center—my first of four. I had sold no art, but people came to sit, talk, share and receive healings. I was sitting with a client, talking, when my mother arrived. She sat down to wait for me. After I walked my client to the door to say goodbye, I turned to see a painful emotional expression on my mother's face. "Why can you not be as nice to me as you are to a stranger?" she asked. No hello. No hug. No movement from her seat. Okay now, let's just go for the jugular.

I have no memory of the conversation that followed. I do remember, however, that my lack-filled apology to her fell short.

After my brother picked her up, I locked the door, put a "closed" sign on the front, and went to sit in meditation. My mother was right. I was nicer to strangers than I was to her. This did not feel good to either one of us. Now that this unspoken secret had been brought to light, most honestly and courageously through my mother, I wanted to know *why*. Why was our relationship like this? Why was I kind, but not to her? Why was I angry with her?

I understood the psychological reasons, how alcohol and her life choices had influenced her relationships. My father was my mother's fourth husband. Her first marriage (at age eighteen) lasted less than three years. Her second husband, to whom she was married less than a year, died in war, leaving her a widow at age twenty-three with a newborn who never met her biological father. At twenty-nine she married her third husband, who abused her. My mother was thirty-three when she married my father. They were together for forty-four years, until his death. Being a physically stunning woman that men had publicly groped, she never knew her worth. You may think this was enough to know. Yet, I felt there was more. More to see, more to understand. I wanted to forgive her, her humanness. She pushed every single button I had. I could not understand her way of being, her lack of security, her need for all she was dependent on, from alcohol and prescription drugs to always being in a palpable defense mode. I wanted to authentically feel love for my mother. I wanted to appreciate her. Perhaps even "like" her. I turned within. Dig deeper, I told myself.

At this time, meditation was my tool for self-discovery. I stated my question and sat in silence awaiting direction. The answer to this question was much more than I had expected or seen before.

I was immediately brought to a different time and space. It was dark—black, really. The void may even be the accurate word. I was standing on the edge of an etheric precipice. No, I did not see it, I could only feel it. I knew because as I was leaning into the openness, I was looking out into space, knowing I was speaking with God. (Yes, I was surprised.) Stars surrounded me. I was planning my next incarnation.

God asked me, "What do you want to learn this time on earth?"

My soul answered. "Number one, to have faith in my healing abilities. For many lifetimes I have failed in not having enough faith in myself as a healer. Number two, to know that skin beauty is not true beauty. Number three, to learn to say no."

This was all news to me. I was present yet also watching and listening. My higher self was speaking, not my human self. At this point, I realized I was no longer in human form. Perhaps it would be called quantum form—my being in multiple ways all at once! I was being given the extraordinary gift of seeing before my time here in this incarnation. I was a light being. Remarkable. Truly, a flicker of light, as were the thousands of others standing behind me. An extraordinary scene I still see in my mind's eye. Thousands of flickering lights, each one a living soul. (I can compare this moment to when I was in the Boston Garden to witness, listen and behold the Dalai Lama. I was fortunate to be sitting very close to the stage. Before his entrance, I stood, turned, and looked at the magnificent sea of humanity which had filled the seats. It is said there were ten thousand people in attendance that evening. It was a breathtaking sight. I remember it as an exceptional moment.)

As I spoke my intentions for my next life on earth, another light being enthusiastically spoke up. (I refer to Neale Donald Walsch's 1998 book, *The Little Soul and the Sun,* for your reading enjoyment; the book had not yet been published and I was not to read it until at least ten years later.)

"I know, I know, I will come back as your mother!" The voice was so excited I cannot express in words her joy. Think of the energy of a five-year-old wanting ice cream. The palpable excitement was real, it was an authentic resonance of *I know how I can help, please let me help!*

"What good will that do?" I asked.

"Well, I will be a physically beautiful woman, an alcoholic plus addicted to prescription drugs. My lack of self-worth will show you that outer beauty is not an answer to happiness. Combined with my lifelong surgeries and health issues, you will see that healing does not take place from anything outside oneself. You will see that these choices are not an answer to curing, or feeling better physically or emotionally. I will be married several times, the last one to your earthly father who will be vaguely inappropriate with you, not directly sexual, but it is in the air. You will have to use your voice. You will learn respect and boundaries from the lack of them. Our family will be financially secure enough for the best of all material things, and you will learn that these too are not an answer to happiness. Due to this awareness, you will grow up to seek what does heal, supporting your journey to remember the innate wisdom of your faith in the power of the Creator. You will claim all of this in your life, expressed through your healing gifts."

As I wept with gratitude because I could not remember ever feeling so loved, I asked this amazing light being, "You are willing to come to Earth to be all this for me? To be someone others do not like?"

For the first time in this earthly existence, my heart center was filled with unconditional love. I somehow knew I could feel how this magnificent light being in human form would not have many friends. She would be a challenging personality. This Light Being stated; *"Of course, I would be honored to be this for you to become all that you are to be."*

At this moment, I knew this light being who would be my earth mother and I had agreed upon a sacred contract. In my present earth form, I realize that we come to Earth to have varied experiences—not good, bad, horrible, or easy. I instantly knew, in human forms, we are willing to be someone who may not appear kind or loving, in order to help others evolve, due to our soul's enormous faith in God. We know this earth experience is all temporary. We choose to incarnate on Earth to have these tactile experiences. I knew in my heart that our greatest teachers were the ones who pushed our buttons, triggered us galore, *loved us deeply,* and loved God beyond any measure, as God loves us. At this moment in time, I understood free will. In an instant, I realized this earth's existence was not all there is. And, of most value, that our souls are immortal.

This experience, which was the first of many alternate reality encounters I have had, taught me and showed me of God's immense love. Coming back into my physical body from this awakened state, I only experienced gratitude for this soul who was my mother. I was overcome with the love I felt, tears poured from me. I was in awe of the incredible web of this sacred existence.

I have never forgotten this experience. It is an unwavering memory in my awareness. This did not change my mother. She was still an alcoholic; she was still the person she came here to be.

Yet, I only grew more empowered. It did change me. Tremendously. I began to extend kindness towards her instead of blame. I felt appreciation instead of impatience. I felt understanding rather than frustration. As I have aged into my sixties, I rarely talk about my mother without tears of gratitude for her being what she was, what she chose to be, for me to become who I am, for I have grown to love myself, to sincerely like myself. It is my steadfast conviction that the holy ripple effect from this altered reality encounter has benefited each client, beloved, and congregant in my life. Every time I sit with a person who has a terminal illness, or is suffering due to their upbringing, or is holding onto childhood anger well into adulthood, I have this amazing truth to share, this incredible experience to speak of, this lesson God gave me to hold onto, to perhaps think of and sit in the vibration of, with and for another person, holding the energy of healing, until they are willing to see their story differently. I know "other" is possible for them. I know that we *can* transcend our human emotions through sacred awareness. I know it for me, and you.

———————

Pivotal moments. The moments that in hindsight we can see we were at a crossroads. These moments shape who we are, who we become. The moments when we went with our gut, said no instead of yes, went right instead of left, took a chance, a risk, a leap into the unknown. The ordinary moments when we were one way before it happened, and another way after the experience. Only we know them. They belong to us. Do you know yours?

7

DIRECT CONTACT

We all have them, unexpected moments that change our entire life, that catapult us in the image we have of ourselves. They seemingly come out of nowhere — yet in hindsight, we can see Divine Intelligence behind the scenes.

~ Deborah Evans Hogan

◆

During the first week of having just moved in with my now-husband Bill, I had scheduled my first evening as part of a séance circle in Salem, Massachusetts. The hostess was an astrologer who had recently visited my gallery/healing center. For over twenty years, she had hosted a weekly séance that was held by invitation only. In other words, she chose you. I said yes.

Other than a Ouija board when I was young (which I believed did spell out messages and was just too weird to keep doing), I had no experience attempting to deliberately contact those who had transitioned. Since my knowledge is that we never die, I rarely use that term. Instead, I use "transitioned." My knowing is that only the form/body dies, not our essence. Our true identity/soul/spirit leaves the physical body from this plane of existence, separating from the ego, and goes home. A Native American teaching is *that the soul is set free.* How beautiful.

Other than the board that talked, I had never purposely chosen to commune with those who had passed. At the Salem séance, seven of us sat around a table with a burning candle, in a dimly lighted room. I was the newbie, as everyone else had been attending for years. Yes, it felt like a movie set *and* it was comfortable, for me. We joined hands, our hostess spoke an invocation, and then we were asked to sit quietly and be open to receiving messages from the beyond. When the time was up, our hostess would invite us to share our messages, if we had any.

Immediately a young boy named Christopher stood to my right, between myself and an older woman, Joanne, who was in her seventies, had been coming to this circle since it began. Christopher was very sweet, very blonde, and very happy to come through. I was not frightened or disturbed. To my astonishment, it felt natural. We communicated telepathically. I saw him as five years old, the age he was when he had left his body and moved from his earthly form. His mother was the woman to my right. He had transitioned when Joanne was in her thirties. He gave me a message for her and then left, as gently as he had appeared.

Coming back to the circle, lights switched on, the hostess asked if anyone had any communications. I turned to my right and gently addressed Joanne, this woman I had just met. I had no idea what I was doing, if I had made it all up or what had just happened. Were we supposed to hear words, see "dead" people, talk with them? Did I do it right? How do I say this—hello, I know we just met, but your deceased child just spoke with me? With deference to what I believed was my ignorance, combined with my faith in the fact I had been invited by a respected astrologer, I spoke up.

Joanne's tears fell rapidly. I remember others' faces at the table fully engaged with our exchange. The hostess had known Joanne for over twenty-five years and knew her as a childless woman. Joanne's pain from her son's death had never been shared with any of these people. She had lived in another state at the time, so she had left that history behind her. I remember Christopher to this day; it is as if it is his gratitude I carry with me. I also remember Joanne's appreciation for having known her child had stood beside her, been in her presence, was existing in other realms. For many years Joanne had come to this weekly séance circle, waiting to hear from her dead son. For me, it was a privilege beyond words.

Why me, you ask? So did I. I was there without any preconceived notions, perceptions, expectations, or beliefs. I carried only openness. I had no resistance. I believe my energy was exactly where I try to be now with every client today: empty—so God can come through.

When I arrived home, I awoke Bill to not only share the experience but give him a "get out of relationship card." This was our first week living together. He had not signed up for this. I told him about my evening. I told him I knew, deep in my heart, this was only the beginning, that there would be more. I had no idea what "more" was. With my wide-open heart, I allowed him the opportunity to leave the relationship. I held no concern, only unconditional love, letting him choose freely. My condo had not yet sold, so it would have been easy to pull the plug on this planning-a-life-together idea. He chose to stay. Honestly, during our years together, as my work shifted, as I changed, as I expanded, I have made this offer to him a few times. Each time I have offered with only love and freedom for him to choose what he truly wants to make him happy in his life. For my mainstream beloved husband, marrying someone with a regular nine-to-five job and health insurance remains only a dream.

Direct contact is not always comfortable. As my life expanded into understanding multidimensional existences, I have experienced a few interesting exchanges. Shortly after a Reiki weekend of classes, I went to bed for a sound night's sleep. In our small apartment on the second floor of an old farmhouse, I was startled from sleep by a floating head. It was a bright red face, and it had wings coming from the back of its skull. Floating there, right in front of me. "No!" Stoically rising from bed, I went into the kitchen, and paced, back and forth, "No, you are *not* allowed to bother me!" I spoke out loud firmly, and feeling surprisingly in charge. I have never seen it since. (This is a universal law—when bothered by a negative energy, as you stand firmly planted in your faith and tell it to leave, *it has to.* This is not about anger or fear, this is about applying law, taking a stance.)

———————————

There was a very lovely time I was meditating at the altar in one of my healing centers when Sathya Sai Baba (a Hindu guru) appeared. He was so kind to come to visit me. I had read of people sharing of his visitations, so I was and am very grateful. Sai Baba was in the flesh. We had no conversation; I have always believed it to be a Darshan (a blessing received by sight through beholding an eminent person) moment. He simply was right there, starring into my eyes with a lovely grin. Shortly after this, I had a call from a healer I knew, asking if she could come to the center and share her adventure of visiting Sai Baba's ashram in India. The next evening, she came to generously share her experience. No fee. A gift. It all came together in twenty-four hours. We called people, put the word out, and had a full house. Before she left, she gave me a package of his vibhuti (sacred ash) as a gift. To this day, although this happened twenty-three years ago, this sacred ash is never used up. Never-ending love from Sai. When we are willing, mystical gifts can be seen each day. (Vibhuti originates in a number of ways: from burnt wood, cow dung, burned bodies from Hindu ritual and/or as Sai Baba manifested it from the air through his hands, as witnessed by many students. I use it for blessings on physical bodies, as in the third eye area during a ritual and on Ash Wednesday. Some people apply it for healing.)

8

JESUS

Verily, verily, I say unto you, He that believeth on me, the works that I do shall he do also; and greater works than these shall he do; because I go unto my Father.

~ John 14:12

♦

Let me share my beliefs concerning Jesus. Jesus was a human man who exemplified faith in God, in the Universe, in the Creator. Personally, I see my belief in Jesus as my bridge to the mystical. I am in partnership with him, and this allows me to know what is possible. He shows me how my faith in God, plus believing in his (Jesus's) existence, allows me to co-create through Universal Law on this earth plane. I consider Jesus my friend, my brother, my teacher, and way-shower. For those who wonder why I am not saying he is the son of God, I believe we *all* are children of God. He knew this, lived this, expressed it, applied it, and believed it more than anyone else—so far. Jesus showed us what the possibilities are when we have faith in the Creator's Power and Presence.

I cannot remember learning about him. I remember seeing Jesus when I was a child playing in the yard. Growing older, I remember shying away from his photos and religious people when they wanted to talk about him. Years passed, and I now love him, know him, trust him, and depend on him. My conversations with him, as well as *A Course in Miracles* (a 1976 book scribed by Helen Schucman) and Julia Ingram's *The Messengers* (1997), certainly have played—and continue to each day—a deep role in my relationship with Jesus.

I believe John 14:12. I believe each of us has the potential to allow what we call miracles in our lives. I believe every single person, if they choose, can be internally guided through Divine Intelligence to achieve their dreams and know great possibilities.

I have met Jesus. The very first time was above a toy store in Marblehead, Massachusetts. A like-minded friend told me a healer from England was seeing clients in the United States. I should not miss her, my friend said, and so I went. It was one of those times you just knew you should say yes. I knew nothing about this healer, I had read nothing about her. I only knew my friend suggested her.

I climbed the old staircase to a small greeting room where I met Lottie, a tiny-framed powerhouse of a woman. With no personal agenda, I opened to what she felt was right for me. Lead the way.

Lottie brought us to another room, where I sat in a chair. I was directed to close my eyes. The next thing I knew, I was sitting on a granite bench, on the top of a knoll looking out over beautiful green hills. Taking in the sunny day, I then noticed Jesus walking up the hill to me. He sat beside me on the bench, to my left. We turned to face one another. I felt deep joy and familiarity. I knew Him, there were no introductions. He took my hands and spoke to me. He told me I was a teacher. I feel He told me other things, but I have no recollection of them. I asked questions, and He answered. I have no memory about what. When Lottie touched my shoulder and called my name to open my eyes, my first thought, other than "wow," was: *A few more minutes please, this was too short a time, I want more time with Him.*

Not asking any questions of me, she led me to the outer reception area, showed me the donation bowl, and said goodbye. Looking at the clock on the wall, I saw over an hour had passed.

This concept of time gets obliterated when crossing realities and having out-of-body experiences.

As I walked outside, I wondered, what *does* one do after they have met and talked with Jesus? This question became my only thought for the day.

Jesus and I met again at Logan airport in Boston. My husband and I were flying out to Arizona for a vacation. The night before our early morning flight, I was in a dream heading down a familiar entrance to a gate at the airport. At the end of the aisle, where passengers had to go either left or right to different gates, Jesus stood directing me to go right, not left. He was smiling, saying hello, and holding an arrow sign pointing right.

I said nothing of my dream to my husband. As we read our gate number and were given directions, I found myself on the exact entranceway I had walked in my dream. Our scheduled gate was to the bottom, on the left. Yup, you got it—at the end of the walkway was an airport sign, redirecting us to the right. They had to change the flight to a different airplane due to something being wrong with the original aircraft.

As we waited to board, I went to the window to silently thank Jesus. I looked at our plane. It had my angel numbers on it: 444. When I see these numbers, I know my angels are in charge, taking care of and surrounding me. Is now the time for me to share that my husband's social security number includes the digits 444?

One Easter morning when I had a public healing center, I held a silent meditation. Only a few came, yet it was a very powerful morning. As I sat in front of the altar in the meditation room with my eyes closed, I was brought to the crucifixion; I was a woman standing in the crowd watching, crying, and heaving for my teacher on the cross. Yet, Jesus also stood beside me as I watched and spoke. "You were there with me. This was my sacred contract. Know that if this had not happened, I would never have been remembered."

When I ended the meditation with the ringing of a singing bowl, I turned to look at my guests—and tears were falling on each face. They knew not why, except that the love they felt in the room was overpowering. With no further explanation, I let it go at that.

My business partner, Darby, an RN as well as energy practitioner, and I had co-created a healing center. We each had individual treatment rooms, a small room as a shop, and one large room for Reiki clinics, teaching, and meditations. One day, a woman unknown to both of us walked into our center. Nancy had come to inquire about a session that would have Darby and I both working on her at once. Except for teaching students, Darby and I had not previously worked together with one client. Nancy had heard about our center and was confident we could help her. Nancy explained to us she felt she had "something" inside her body that needed to come out. This "something" was taking over her life. It felt negative to her and was preventing her from being a good mother to her child, and her marriage was in trouble as well. She was willing to pay the joint price we quoted her. We all realized we were taking a chance; this was new territory for each of us. Darby and I avoided the word "exorcism."

Setting up in the large meditation room, Darby stood on one side of the table and I was opposite of her. We proceeded to do what we normally do: Reiki, Polarity, laying on of hands, and the addition of silent prayer from me. Nancy began to move. She uttered guttural sounds. As if that was not enough, to our pure shock, the table raised off the floor. Wide-eyed, Darby and I starred at one another. While we kept our hands on our client, silently mouthing to one another, "the table is off the floor," I began saying "Jesus" under my breath. Because this was beyond our usual treatment, I had to hand it all over to Jesus. Soon, Nancy relaxed and the table stilled.

I do not remember Nancy's post-session remarks, but I do remember that Darby and I did not talk much about it. We *knew* something had taken place, but what? We both believed in healing, no matter what someone chose to call it. I do not doubt in my mind and heart that something left Nancy's energy field during that session.

As it came to pass, we never heard from Nancy again, that I know of. But in keeping an eye out for her, I learned she was an elder in her church, heading up committees, still married, and happily a mother. Even though I did not see Jesus this time, I know beyond a doubt He was present.

———————

After I completed writing this story about Nancy, I wondered how she was. I asked Spirit to remind me of her real name, which I could not remember, and to please shine some light on how her life was now. I had moved from the town she lived in and where our healing center was seven years ago. The next day I went on Facebook and a client had posted about the death of her dear friend. It was Nancy. Nancy had been well respected and loved in the town, was happily married with two children. She had simply gone to her room to nap, and never woke up.

9

POWER OF PRAYER

Getting out of our own way is a spiritual practice.

~ Deborah Evans Hogan

•

have witnessed answered prayer thousands of times. I depend on it, often throughout just one day. Some are selfish little prayers, others are critical requests, yet they each are an acknowledgment of the available Divine support for us in this physical form. How does prayer work? Do we know? I believe it is a creative calling within the Great Architect's energetic framework of Its Divine Creation, through an individual's alignment (according to law, belief, allowance, faith) with all that is. Through one's vibrational alignment it is so, it is revealed. This has absolutely nothing to do with an outsider judging you or deciding if you are worthy. It is the Creator's law that it is done to us and through us according to *our* faith.

As many people do, I have learned that when I get out of the way, when I stop trying to control, micromanage, fix, force or go against anything, God steps in and grace appears. Ease happens. Prayer helps me to uncling from how I think a situation should be handled, in order to turn it over to God so it *can* be handled. In prayer, I am paying attention to what I call truth. I live by the Universal metaphysical law that energy flows where our attention goes. I teach that whatever you pay attention to, you receive more of, no matter if your attention comes from fear or love; *it is all attention. Your energy is dancing with the energy of whatever is your focus.* This is an energetic merging, a vibrational dance, an intertwining of qualities.

Let's discuss how to pray and types of prayer for a moment. First off, as I would think this needs no explanation, *prayer is not, never is, never will be, or has been, about wishing or begging for harm to another.* If you find yourself feeling like you wish to pray for harm, go pray for forgiveness. Now, from this author's viewpoint, every intentional prayer should be spoken aloud. This is not for God's benefit or to impress another human with your words, but for *your* benefit. As we sit in this field of our spoken word, a transformation takes place within us. When we shift from silently hearing words in our head, as if in secret, to speaking them (activating our throat chakra—our power center), hearing them, and listening to them; our thoughts, perceptions, and vibrations are shifted. Speak aloud your prayers, feel them resonate in your body, allowing the energy of the spoken word to help vibrationally align your cells with your prayer, through your faith. When you are fully without resistance you will witness your word manifested in form.

I choose from two types of prayer—there is *asking for,* and *affirming what is.* I have witnessed both to be successful. I prefer one instead of the other for different reasons at different times, based on my emotional status. In asking for, I feel it is from a place of acknowledging the power I am praying to is greater than myself and, at this moment, I feel helpless. Helpless to advise, helpless to know what is best. There may be such chaos that it is overwhelming. Most often in this space, I ask Jesus for God's mercy to pour down and through the person or experience I am praying about. I am laying it at the altar. Without any doubt, in this energy, I know it will be done, can be done; as long as I am out of the way. I get out of the way *through* total surrender to God.

Affirming prayer is what I learned through Unity and Science of Mind teachings. In this sensibility of praying, we are One with God. For me, it comes from a space of empowerment, of full recognition as a child of God, as in Oneness, non-duality, no separation. In the energetic framework of this form of praying, I am already aligned with infinite possibilities and am affirming by stating, not asking for, Divine intervention for support. In my alignment attained from the words, my frequency is raised, and the desired outcome is reached.

Within two months of moving to our present home, we received a letter in the mail from a corporate mediator who was employed by a gas company conglomerate trying to get approval for a pipeline through our town. I knew about this effort due to the protests, town meetings, and a local bookstore that served as a center for activists working to prevent the pipeline.

The letter said that we could expect a one-time offer for the purchase of our home. If we refused, our home would then be taken by eminent domain. The pipeline was to go directly through our newly acquired property. I took a deep breath and called the mediator, who suggested he was willing to come to our home to answer any questions. No thank you, I said, as I had only one question: Did the previous owners know about this? Silence. "Yes, they did," he admitted. I centered myself, thanked him, hung up, and prayed.

As my husband and I sat with our options, it was very clear to me the only choice I had was to hand this over to God. I had to trust what I call my higher power because I refuse to dance with anything negatively. How did I do this? It was the simplest prayer yet: "God, this is Yours."

I had to remove myself from any actions, worries, concerns, or fears. I refused to be in the way of God. I gave it to God. My husband had to select his own way; attending town meetings was his choice. We did agree that being upset with the previous owner was not an answer. Perhaps they sold us the house because they did know. It is done. Where could chasing this conversation lead us? I told myself God did not bring us here to take this home away from us. For me, going to protests or paying attention to any fear or blame concerning this situation were not options, because they would only bring more fear. If I ever had to go by faith, this was the time.

I am not an activist at all. I may be a prayer warrior, but I am not a protestor. I consciously choose to go *with* something, never against anything. I realize that activism has made a difference in our country as well as positive changes in the lives of many. I prefer to pray, get out of the way, and focus on what I wish to see, not the fear of a potential anything. This works miracles in my daily life and as far as I can see, in the lives of my clients. If I believed their stories could not be changed when they came to me for healing, how could healing ever take place? I would be adding to the problem, not offering a solution. I believe in the strength of God more than the evidence of pain or illness. I believe love heals, not anger or any level of fear. My faith must and does override x-rays, diagnosis, prognosis, and mindsets. God is greater.

When I would go into a local shop and found myself stopped to talk about the pipeline at the checkout, my faith had to come into play; I am trusting God. When I went into the bookshop and was asked to sign petitions, I chose to gently explain my stance. I appreciated what they were doing because they were doing what they believed in, but my way was different.

It was a month or more before the pipeline that was projected to go through our town was canceled. Do I believe it was my faith? Absolutely. Do I believe the protestors made the difference? Absolutely. Can it not be an either-or? I tell you what, I would never want to try to fix, heal or cure any big, life-threatening, value-challenging *anything* without putting it in God's hands. In this case, I do not ignore the human aspects of town hall meetings, community education, and peaceful activism; God is there, too.

Other than a fiftieth wedding anniversary renewal of vows, the first wedding I officiated was my niece's in Ohio. My sister's family lived in a private golf course community. The wedding was in their backyard. No, it was not small. They had set up several tents of various sizes and purposes. Everything about it was stunning.

My sister had me stay at her friend's home, still within the compound. It was perfect for me to have privacy away from the wedding hubbub. The night before my niece's nuptials, I asked my host about driving to my sister's home on the other side of the complex in the morning. Will there be traffic? They assured me it was not an issue. The golfers take the main entrance gate in, which is not near their home, and no trucks are allowed in the residential part of this very upscale environment. All deliveries, they told me, went in a back way to the country club building itself. Little if any traffic.

My wedding morning prayers were many. My first large wedding *and* it was family. I asked for a sign that I was doing what I was supposed to. A sign that I was following God's direction. I prayed for a beautiful day and ceremony, knowing grace in all things.

I can still remember getting in my car, robe ready to go, service prepared in my new leather-bound journal, calming my anticipatory nerves through more prayer. As I went around the curve at the end of my host's street, heading to an intersection, there it was. A massive multi-wheeler truck with the huge letters **G.O.D.** on the side, with the tag line, **G**uaranteed **O**vernight **D**elivery. (Which, of course, I have never seen since.)

No trucks allowed in this area, huh? Thank you, God. Nerves calmed.

After my father transitioned in the fall of 1996, my mother and I hit a wall. Talk about crossroads. After forty-four years of marriage, she was broken, devastated, lost, and alone, except for their dog, Brownie. During my mother's last few months on earth, Spirit came through more than once directing me, "go to Florida." I went. I found my mother in bed from the flu, but it had turned into alcohol detox, for she was too weak to get out of bed and get a drink.

This was a very hard time in both our lives. She was flat out refusing any help. She would not agree for me to call her counselor, or go see or even let me call the doctor. At one point when she made it out of her bed to the dining room, we had our first-ever argument. I was utterly lost. We yelled. We were actually in each other's faces. She screamed at me. This was not anything we had ever done before. I had never experienced verbal arguing with anyone. No one in our family did this. Neither one of us was a yeller, or provoker, or arguer; instead we would stifle, we would sit in silence. We were well-behaved New England WASPS. My mother climaxed her anger by slapping my face, then struggled to go back to bed. Devastated, I went to my room to pray.

I remember being awake all night, talking with God, my angels, pretty much anyone who would listen. In the early morning hours, I cried out to God. I needed help. "We need Your Divine assistance." It was one of those surrender cries when we have nothing left, nowhere to go, not another ounce of ideas, not one more prayer, not one spoken word left, the on-my-knees-I-give-up-kind-of-cry. A come-to-Jesus experience.

Then it happened. (Please, stay with me here. I am sharing this encounter with you, an experience that happened to me, that to this day is at the top of my list of the most woo-woo, weird, unexplainable, amazing things ever.) The ceiling turned into white light. It started as a circle from the center, then expanded into pure radiance. Imagine the ceiling turning into a high-wattage lightbulb. I watched intensely, taken in by my real-life Spielberg moment. The ceiling had gone away and the light was unlike anything I had ever seen or imagined. I do not remember breathing. Awestruck. The light itself did not light up the room, which remained in the pre-dawn darkness, but the ceiling was glowing! I have no idea how long this lasted. I do know it ended when I heard my mother's voice screaming my name from the kitchen. I found her huddled over the sink, her feeble hands supporting her in place, shaking with age and alcoholism. "I will do whatever you want me to do," she said. Can I get a hallelujah? Answered prayer—a most magnificent and glorious event to witness.

This does not mean she became a different person or got sober. My mother never got sober. She remained determined to get her scotch, even if it meant having her friends sneak it into the house in a little brown bag after I had given all the bottles and cases of liquor away. (This would happen right in front of me, too.) It does mean the counselor was called. It does mean a softness was revealed that allowed us to admit my mother to the hospital.

My prayers to God are not always calm, pretty, pleasant, or patient. Yes, sometimes my humanness reigns and I let the Universe know my stance.

Years ago, after I had opened my gallery and before it was in full force as a healing center, I was down to very little cash. I had no idea how I was going to come up with the rent or pay for groceries.

I remember driving to work, angry and crying. I was tired and no doubt a bit scared. I did not yet have the calm security about God that I carry today. It was still in the developmental stages. In my car,

I yelled. I demanded that something *had* to give. I needed money and I needed it now. Something God, something, please, help.

And then I let it go. It is a most palpable sensation. We know that feeling when we un-cling and give a worry to God. It is true that sometimes we have to be in quiet desperation, on our knees, to let go and let God. We have to be in so much fear we cannot depend on anything else but Spirit, to be so exhausted from trying to control that nothing is left in us but surrender. *Then, we are out of our own way.*

The gallery phone rang shortly after I arrived at my desk. My mother's voice was on the other end with the news. She and my father had decided to gift each child the maximum yearly financial gift of ten thousand dollars. They felt they might as well watch us enjoy it before they died.

At this point, I was in awe again. I doubt my parents had my car bugged, nor had I told anyone else of my financial dilemma, only God.

Answered prayer, an effect of our faith. The secret to successful prayer may be to realize that we need to talk God into nothing—what we are doing is talking ourselves into accepting something. Our affirming of potential good opens doorways to receiving good. As we build our faith through noticing positive good in our lives, we eventually become more and more accepting of good. In other words, each time we notice the positive or the slightest blessings, or acknowledge God working on our behalf, our inner vibration is raised, our frequency changes, and increased good is revealed. *We accept (receive) only what we believe is possible.*

A friend Susan once wrote seven of her friends to invite them into a private prayer circle for her health. She chose to not post on social media or tell anyone else but the seven of us she shared her intimate request with. She had been diagnosed with a cancerous tumor in her stomach. Mind you, she had already beat cancer once before and was still wanting to only implement alternative methods for her healing.

This description of a five-part prayer treatment is from the original email I shared with the prayer circle. This form of prayer comes from the Science of Mind teaching, as it was taught to me. This is referred to as a five-part prayer treatment, with "treatment" being the operative word. *This is to be spoken out loud, so the one praying the treatment can embody the vibration of the declarations.* The belief is we are *one,* the one receiving is healed as we come into alignment with the desire. As you feel your loved one brought into your heart of Oneness, a Holy Connection is ignited. How? Your loved one is brought into your inner vision as you declare aloud. There will emerge a clarity within you of your loved one's presence, as the Divine Truth expresses that we are *one.* We each make up a part of the cosmic whole. Each step allows for deeper intensity. Each step is to be completed and palpably known within you before you go on to the next step. Below the bold underlined text is the spoken title of the step, the remaining language is up to the one initiating the prayer treatment.

1. **GOD IS ALL THERE IS. There is nothing else but God.** All things, all creatures are made of God. We are each part of the Infinite Oneness of Light, unified from Source. God is love, joy, faith. God is the birdsong, the words of Rumi, the sun, the moon, and the stars. God holds the planets in the universe, the perfect balance of nature, the rhythms of our pulses. God is the luscious smell of Susan's grandbabies, the flowers from the earth, the love I feel when I am in holy connection with another being.

2. **GOD AND I ARE ONE.** Like the drop of water from the ocean, I am a drop of God. There is no separation. The God that I am sees the God in all Life. As my heart opens to *all*

Divine Possibilities, I am embodying the Infinite and Eternal Light, which is Source, God, Creator, the Great Is-ness. I relish in the vibration of Godliness, the juiciness of Love, the eternalness of Bliss, the bodacious-ness of Being, the pure Joy of God.

3.   **THIS PRAYER IS FOR SUSAN.** God is Susan's body. God my mind, God my heart, and God my spirit. Wherever an awareness of God is, there is no disease, imbalance, or lack. God is Susan. Susan is God. Susan's beautiful vibration is lifted by the love which surrounds her each day, in every moment, as every breath—by my mind and her magnificent mind, as all the Grandmothers who eternally have their hands and hearts upon her, by the realms, layers, and rings of Love and Light which surround and are our universe. I see Susan as the Light of God which she is. Her magnificent soul is vibrating at divine health and wholeness. The Light of God penetrates every cell of her being and transforms anything unlike itself to Itself. *Nothing* is too difficult for God. God is the ultimate white hat! God has ridden in and never left! God is all-encompassing, and the perfection of the Light is filling Susan's body, mind, belly, every organ and creating miracles. There are so many miracles the doctors are blown away! This is an opportunity for the medical world to behold God in action! Susan is free of disease, free of any old thoughts, stories, or vibrations of lack. Susan is surrounded by her angelic force, by the Masters, by Beings of Light and Wisdom, all of curing and healing, and we are each overcome by this experience of prayer!

4.   **I GIVE THANKS.** Thank you, God, for this time of pure bliss, knowing, and faith. May this vibration stay with me, be as me and fill me—and as Susan and I are One, she is also filled. Thank you.

5.   **I RELEASE.** I release this prayer to you, God, to the Universe of Infinite Light, to be carried and completed. It is done!

Susan loved the prayer; it resonated for her and she said it daily. One can own any prayer by changing the pronouns to "me," "myself," or "I am." I also did this prayer as distant work each morning and whenever Spirit guided me.

You may want to know that Susan was initially brought to the hospital for an unusual bout of dehydration. They discovered this tumor indirectly, by what some may call a miracle.

After receiving this prayer, in a few weeks, Susan called me to say she had gone back to the doctor to receive an update on her scans as well as his suggestions for treatment. Her physician sat behind his desk, as Susan described it, looking down at his paperwork in a quiet, quizzical manner. He looked up at her and said, "I am not sure how this happened, Susan, but there is no sign of cancer in your body. Whatever you are doing, keep doing it. I do not need to see you again." Her laugh of joy was utter fabulousness.

A woman I met many years ago when I was a regular guest minister at her church in Rhode Island contacted me for prayer and support via email, as she had moved to Arizona and I was in Massachusetts. Leslie was a woman in her late sixties with long-term health issues including an autoimmune label and heart issues that were calling for surgery. She claimed the heart issues were hereditary. This was her belief.

When we spoke, Leslie told me of the diagnosis. Her doctors had voiced grave concerns. She was having a meeting with them soon, then a procedure to assess blockages, then an actual surgery on her right aorta valve. Since moving to Arizona, Leslie had not yet found a church community for spiritual support. Her reaching out to me was her way of wanting to be reminded of what she already knew.

In our phone session, we spent an hour applying prayer, through the Science of Mind five-part treatment described above as well as my work. Initially, she was on a bit of a gerbil wheel of fear, and it's easy to see why, when the medical world was supplying her with information about great risks, including death during surgery. At the end of our conversation, she felt better. Her energy had drastically shifted. More hopeful, more positive. The next morning, I was moved by Spirit to write out more words, affirmations, and prayers for her. In texts and emails, she reported using all we spoke of and all I sent her. Calm was newly present. She easily aligned with the phrase, "God's got this."

The meeting with her team of doctors before the procedure and surgery of this medically complicated case was interesting, as Leslie reported to me, and I quote: "They were telling me I could die on the table, Rev. Deb—and because my response was not fear, they looked at me and asked, *Are you understanding what we are telling you?*" She assured them she did and went on to explain her faith in God had quelled any fears she had.

Two days later Leslie texted me. "The procedure went very well. No artery blockages. I am doing my affirmations! All is falling into place." (The blockages were assumed due to her history. Also, if I remember correctly, they had seen calcification before, but this was not seen now.)

Day of surgery—three days later, on the day of surgery. I sent prayers, texts, and love reminders. I had no idea when I would hear from her again, what with ICU to follow, a difficult surgery, etc. I handed it all to God.

The day after surgery. (This was directly copied from her text.) "The operation was a success. I feel terrific and the doctor said there was no complication at all and right before I was put under anesthesia, I saw your face, my Goddess, and Archangels Gabriel and Michael and then I dozed right off! Thank you for everything! I am whole! In the hospital overnight, but if there were any complications I would have had to stay in ICU, and of course, I DO NOT!"

Later that day she wrote me this: "Another good news is I am going to be discharged today."

Five days later, "I went to the cardiologist follow-up today and he says he is so amazed that I was out of the hospital in one night considering all the problems I have. He repeated the operation was so successful! He said even people without other health issues stay at least two nights."

An incredible experience. God revealed.

I had been uncomfortable for days. My lower belly was speaking to me. As I was in my mid-sixties, and had not been to a gynecologist for many years, my mind jumped on the gerbil wheel of fear. Three nights in a row my husband and I sat together in the wee hours on our living room couch, assuring ourselves of my truth and faith. I reached out to a handful of close friends to ask for prayer. I had never been on the gerbil wheel before. This was new to me. I did not like it. In my ministry, I had counseled many through fear of the unknown, but being here, in this place of allowing fear to run my mind, desperately seeking my faith which was hidden beneath fearful thoughts was a humbling experience.

After a pelvic exam revealed nothing unusual, a transvaginal ultrasound was ordered. Prayers were showering me. I was constantly reminding myself of what I knew, how healthy I was, how my body knows to be aligned with my highest good. On my drive to the hospital for the ultrasound, my phone rang. A dear God sister who was in between flights as she traveled throughout the Midwest called to check in with me. Perfect timing. God always knows. I explained how I was feeling, and she very calmly asked, "Why do you think you are having this experience?"

It was as if the light in my head went on and everything cleared. Divine clarity. The knowing of these words flowed from my heart like an epiphany. I answered, "Oh, so I can have true compassion for my clients, my beloveds, I now understand the gerbil wheel of fear!" And it left. I felt the heaviness from the right side of my belly leave my body. All discomfort, pain, anything of concern went with it. Truly, I was experiencing a miracle. Only God could reveal such a palpable instant healing.

I arrived at the hospital calm and in as much peace as I had not known in days. It was an invasive test, but somehow tranquility prevailed until I got back in my car to call my husband. I ranted about the test, all in human humor. As I neared home I prayed aloud in my car, affirming all was well, giving thanks to God. I was preparing to turn left when a car drove directly in front of me from the right with this license plate: THKUGD.

Talk about linear validation of answered prayer!

Initially, a small cyst on my right ovary had been revealed, which carried no immediate medical concerns, but the request for a second transvaginal ultrasound in six months as a follow-up had been made. This test revealed it was not an ovarian cyst but a follicular cyst (not to be seen in a postmenopausal woman, which I was) that had shrunk to half its initial size. Unless symptoms started up again, there was no need for me to come back. It was headed in the right direction. I have had no issues since.

10

TRUSTING GOD – HOLY HINDSIGHT

Those who leave everything in God's hand
will eventually see God's hand in everything.

~ Unknown

◆

As the gallery shifted into being a healing center, each day random people came to sit, talk, be. Clients would come for Reiki sessions: simple, less than an hour, laying on of hands. Migraines went away, lung tissues were growing back after surgery, pain was no longer causing discomfort. I was pretty amazed. Holy Spirit energy was filling up my life. It was quite a remarkable time. Like today, I felt then and still do, that each day I have a front-row seat to watch God in action. Each day, I have the immense gift of seeing the effects of faith, the opulence of an infinite Universe bringing to and through us what is possible with an open mind and heart. I wanted more.

One day after closing the gallery, I went to the beach for a walk, to pray for more. What was "more" to me? I wanted to see mermaids swimming, or behold a client walk after being paralyzed. I don't remember what else I asked for, but I do remember the passion from which I asked. I wanted something big. I wanted to see an undeniable miracle. I still can see myself walking the majesty of Plum Island at dusk, being vocal to God, to the Universe, to let me see more. I asked for something indisputable, that I would unquestionably know was a miracle of Divine intervention. No mermaids came to me. Disappointed, I found my car and drove home.

Entering the kitchen of our small apartment, our cat made it known she was hungry. I opened her evening meal via the metal pull on the flip-top can—and sliced my index finger wide open to the bone. Quite a sight for one who has no surgical training! I looked down at my left-hand index finger and saw the bone. Blood was pouring out, yet I was stunned at how strikingly white the bone was, sliced directly on the inside of the top joint. All I could think was, *I meant this to happen to someone else. Not me.* Obviously, in looking at my finger, I was not clear enough with the powers that be. Without stating it, I assumed my desire to see an undeniable miracle would happen to another, and that I would be a bystander, a witness. Clarity, Deborah, clarity.

Finding a clean white towel, I called for Bill, who ran to the kitchen and stood watching me for a moment, then stating in known defeat, "We're not going to the hospital, are we?" I realized this was a medical emergency, but I also knew this experience was exactly what I had asked for. The joke was on me.

Bill and I reached a compromise that I would sit up in bed to sleep, as he stayed awake right beside me in case I hemorrhaged onto the bed and he had to call an ambulance. (His words.) My hand cradled on a pillow, surrounded with crystals, I immediately began applying Reiki to my finger. After a bit, the bleeding stopped, but bending my finger at all, which happened naturally for the cut was at the joint, re-opened the delicate freshly sliced skin. I asked what I could do, and I was guided to use an etheric metal finger brace. I had seen them in pharmacies. I visualized the brace and placed it on my finger using nonphysical tape to hold it in place. I saw it so, and it was so, and it worked perfectly.

The next morning, with the brace still in place, my finger had not bent at all. The skin was already rebuilding. Later that day my son had a chiropractic appointment, which I took advantage of by casually asking the doctor what he thought regarding my finger. After he asked where the bandage was, and why it was not covered, he stated, "Oh, you sliced a tendon, you'll never have feeling in that finger again." I am an Aries who also has faith that my body knows how to heal—go ahead, tell me I can't or won't or I am not able to, and watch what happens.

A day or two later, my finger showed signs of infection with redness and heat. More Reiki. Within a week the cut was healed enough for me to see clients and gently lay my hand on their bodies. This experience stayed alive in me for over a year, as this finger became my private weather station. An ache was my first sign of rain or snow. Looking at this finger right now, I am humorously in awe of innate Divine Perfection, of what we are created from. I have no scar and total feeling. I certainly did learn to be more explicit when inviting Spirit to intervene, and for whom.

From summer 1996 until spring 1997, I was pummeled with spiritual character builders, or as my ministerial mentor called them, opportunities for God.

One month during the early summer of 1996, I did not have enough money in my bank account to pay the rent on my gallery/healing center. When I had opened this venture, I had promised God that if I ever could not pay the rent, I would close my business without any whining, any doubt, any questions. I keep my covenants with God. When I gave my notice on the lease, the landlord was willing to do whatever it took for me to stay, but I insisted on trusting God.

Closing the gallery was painful. I had built a reputation in the healing arts, and from this had been on the front page of the local newspaper six times in the four years we were open. I had sold very little art even though we had been on the back page of the Sunday

Boston Globe Magazine several times, having one of the writers as a local fan of the gallery. I kept hearing; "I made a promise with God. This is it." I checked my account again, and it was true, not enough funds to manage this month's rent.

I remember the day I cleared the final artful pieces out of the thousand-square-foot space. I locked the door behind me. Standing in front of the hundred-year-old factory building, admiring my beautiful purple and red sign beckoning others to enter, I said thank you and goodbye. I drove home. I wailed all the way. At home, I stepped into the shower and wailed some more. My heart chakra hurt; it was physically painful. I crossed my arms and held them high across my chest and sobbed. I just wanted to let it all out.

I set up an office at home to see my healing clients. The art gallery was history.

A week later I received a call from the bank's accounting department. They had made an error. They called to apologize and make me aware that *somehow* (no linear explanation from them), my credit card payments from customers for the previous month had not gone into my account. I actually had plenty of money to cover the rent.

You ask, how did I not know this? Well, I told myself my calculations were off. I was too emotional and distraught; I had made an error. I would find it later, my mind said. My father had been president of this bank my entire childhood. I had grown up there and knew many of the employees as well, as I had worked at this bank for a few years in my twenties. I trusted them. I mean, they know more than me, right? Was I mad at the bank? No, I was only in awe of God. I trusted the promise I had made with God; if I did not have enough money to pay the rent, I would leave. In that covenant, I gave God something to work with. Somehow, for a not-yet-understood reason, this had happened. I chose to trust Spirit, and that one day, all would be revealed.

Bill and I had been planning our wedding for September 1996. We were renting the second-floor apartment of a farmhouse and, being friends with the owners, we were planning a small outdoor celebration on the land. One day while I was working from my home office, I had a feeling, an intuitive hit, to cancel our wedding plans. I had no valid linear reason. I was into cake tasting. Nothing was wrong. I just "heard" the inner guidance, "for now, cancel your wedding." I approached Bill, who was getting used to me following my instincts, and he agreed that this was a non-issue, we could plan it for another time. Okay, done. Trusting Spirit.

My father passed on September 8, 1996.

Mother's cancer came back from remission two weeks later. My life became filled with phone calls and visits to her Florida home.

My father-in-law passed on October 30, 1996.

Our cat passed on October 31, 1996.

Creating space for my mother to come live with us, we moved to a larger home in a new town in March 1997. Long-distance nursing care was challenging, she was lonely, and together we decided this was the best option.

In moving furniture around in the room that was to be my mother's, I was guided,(Spirit directs, I listen), to turn on the radio. Our radio was always tuned to a local rock station. I then heard from Spirit my mother would not be moving up to New England with us. I was busy getting this room and our new home ready to welcome her. Confused by Spirit's guidance, I sat down, asking what to do next. Immediately, right on time, "Mack the Knife," a 1959 Bobby Darin hit, came on the rock station. This zippy melody was my parent's favorite song to dance to. It didn't matter where they were, when it came on, they rose, embraced, and danced. Dancing was always their happy place. It felt to me my father was letting me know of a greater plan. I then heard, "She needs to die in her own home." Spirit was very clear. "Your mother is not moving here."

In our evening phone call, my mother told me just that. She had decided she did not want to move. I let her know I understood. Your own home simply feels good, secure, and safe. No apologies needed. We will make it work.

In the next few weeks, Bill and I decided to get married. It felt like the right time. A minister friend could be at our home the following weekend. I wrote the service. My son would be our witness. When we went to apply for our marriage license (in the town we had recently moved to, where my ancestors had landed from Ireland), we opened one of the very old antique registration books from the 1880s, found in the town hall record vault. I randomly opened it to the exact page of two of my paternal ancestors' wedding registrations, in their handwriting. A positive blessing indeed.

My mother always believed a woman had to be married to be happy. It was her generation plus her insecurities. On the day of our wedding, I heard the guidance, "go to Florida. Now. Your mother can die a happy woman, you are married." Spirit made it clear that my getting married allowed my mother to let go, to surrender, to go home to be with Dad. My birthday is April 4. We were married on April 5. My maternal grandmother's birthday was April 6. I flew to Florida on the seventh. That evening as I rubbed oils on my mother's back and neck, it was obvious her cancer had spread, as lumps were everywhere. I called in hospice. Even though I was a trained hospice volunteer, had worked in geriatric healthcare, and had been with many as they transitioned, it was important for me to be my mother's daughter at this time.

I called my sister and half-siblings. I found myself saying, "She will be making her transition within two weeks, so if you want to say goodbye, come now." The words that come from our mouths when we have turned our lives over to Spirit can even surprise ourselves. On the eve of April 13, at 9:00 p.m., my mother told me she would be gone in twelve hours. She went home to the Light on April 14, 1997 at 8:14 a.m. Forty-five minutes remained until 9 a.m. She made it just under twelve hours. One week since I had arrived. Seven months since my dad's passing through the veil and ten days before his birthday on April 24.

If I still had owned my art gallery/healing center throughout these tumultuous months, I never could have spent as much time caring for, supporting, being with, and loving on our families. There would have been angst, regret, and hard choices. Instead, there was freedom, support, and love. I listened to Spirit. I trusted God. I do not have one iota of regret about closing the gallery or postponing our wedding. In trusting the urges, the downloads, my inner gut, my belief and faith in a Higher Power than I, life was filled with grace, opportunities to feel God, and yes, love. Divine perfection reigned. *As we trust God, doubts causing any resistance are removed.* This awareness is invaluable.

———————

Trusting God is not easy. Let's face it, we humans like to see something before we believe it. Trusting what we cannot see is asking a lot of you, I realize. But you have my promise, it works and it is worth it. To look back and say, "oh, I asked for that" or "wow, I shifted that thought and then it happened" is glorious! Every single day I call myself back to what I teach, to trust what I know. When clients come to me with a medical diagnosis, I have to be in a space and in faith that I know beyond doubt healing is possible. I know beyond doubt that if you are reading this, you were called here by Divine invitation, no matter how this book fell into your hands.

For me, the big stuff is easy. I go directly to my faith. The little stuff, like the formatting of a manuscript on the computer, I have to hear myself whining before I stop and tell myself a different story. I admit, eventually I do. Instead of saying I do not know how to do something, I remind myself I am smart, I know enough about the computer, I am capable of figuring it out—and *then* all is seen and made right! Trust is knowing that everything is here before us, we just do not see it right now. Claiming it is a sign of devotion. The answer is always somewhere. Remain faithful, and it is revealed.

11

DEATH AND DYING

An awake heart is like a sky that pours light.

~ Hafiz

◆

Death and dying. Honestly, this is a favorite subject of mine. I have supported many as they have crossed through the veils. Some call a person who does this a *transition doula*. I love this name. Death, in the traditional sense, does not exist for me. I choose to say transition, as in transitioning from one home to another, from one reality to another. I have spoken with, seen, felt and communicated with too many people who are said to have died to think of our lives as finite.

To me, death to our True Identity, our essence, is nonexistent. Death is only to the human form on the earth plane. In all that I have perceived, the eternalness of our spirit is what I know to be true. Walking another home, being a transition doula, is the highest calling I have experienced.

There is nothing more intimate than being with another human as they leave their earth body. There are no deeper conversations, nothing more precious, and nowhere is there more love present in our human experience than with another being who is transitioning.

I have experienced poignant, touching exchanges and even hysterical laughter. Helen made me laugh. We had a previous relationship as she had been a weekly client once upon a time. When she was in her late eighties, I had been coming a few days a week for three weeks to her home, where she lived with her daughter and son in law. The day the hospice bed arrived, Helen and I sat in the kitchen and talked. Helen was a toughie. A straight shooter. She wanted to talk politics, but I said, "Anything but that!"

"Okay, let's talk about me dying," she stated in a snarly "show and tell me" voice.

I began to share what was happening. I explained that her ego was separating from her physical body, that the hands of her late husband would be coming through a thin veil to reach for her and walk her home, and that she could look for him. I explained what heaven was like, that it was so very beautiful, and she will feel enormous love. I shared that she may rest for a while upon arrival, but that she will be able to contact her daughter after some rejuvenation, as long as her daughter is not too sad, for that would block Helen from her. I explained to Helen that she will not be far from us, that she will be right here near us, just in another reality.

When I was done talking, she looked at me and said, "Geez, Deborah, you make it sound like a ******** vacation."

As was Helen's way, she took her sweet time to let go, but it was a peaceful journey. As in many families, her daughter struggled with "why is it taking so long." We transition according to our inner clock and no one else's.

Transitioning is, to me, the most personal journey we take. People always ask me when their loved one will pass, and other than in a few intimate circumstances, it is not easy to say. Even though someone appears ready, many factors can affect it. My experience has taught me a few things.

1. If fear or resistance is in the room of your dying loved one, it makes it difficult for a person to leave their bodies. This is why, when the family member who has been sitting by the bed for days crying and feeling anxious and sad finally goes home to shower, their loved one "dies." *I only left the room for an hour, she said. I missed it!* No, actually what you did was give your loved one the space to leave.

2. The most difficult transitions I have witnessed are of those who have controlling personalities. It is very difficult to witness. A peaceful transition requires total surrender to a power greater than I.

3. Your loved one hears everything in the room. Choose your conversations thoughtfully.

4. To me, when a person leaves their body, it looks like a grey mass of energy. This happens moments to forty-eight hours before a person takes their final breath. The last breaths are mechanical to the physical earth body.

A profound gift my mother gave me after her transition home is the single most impactful experience affecting my spiritual beliefs, my understanding of life, my ministry, and my faith. The day after her transition, a call from the funeral home invited me to sit with my mother's body before the cremation. Being with loved ones when they die is a beautiful gift. I find this a profound privilege. The birthing process of the soul going home to the Light is intimate beyond words. Even though I had been with many through their dying process, I had never sat alone with a body after the fact.

My mother's body was beautifully presented in the two-piece navy outfit we had chosen. I sat to her right. This body, perfectly coifed, placed on a white sheet, hygienically laid on a medical gurney, was not my mother. Starring at this body, I was trying to find her. I could feel her, I knew she was in the room. Her essence was profoundly present to me. Yet, as I looked at this empty container, this human body, I knew she was no longer in there. Like a three-year-old, I started laughing, and I poked her cheek. My laughter reverberated in the large empty room with a sterilized tiled floor. *My God! You are still here. I feel you. I hear you... but you are not associated with this body.* A profound experience of knowing, without doubt, that we are *not* our human form. We *are* pure consciousness in these instruments, these homes, these vessels. We are Spirit, we are souls, we are pure Light. We are part of the Divine and the Divine is part of us. My mother, in that room as present consciousness, was indisputable. There was and is no doubt in my heart or mind her True Identity still exists. She simply had moved out of that body.

This awareness that we are spiritual beings had been my intellectual knowing for many years. This was the only choice that made any sense to me, that we are souls, residing in these instruments, that we are not the body. This private, holy moment with my mother unquestionably eliminated any doubt I had left in me. Such freedom to know we thrive. We continue. Eternal life.

———————————

Yes, I had spoken with the dead before. Yes, I had seen those who had transitioned. And even so, this moment was life-changing for me. Perhaps because it was personal, palpable, and tangible—this moment changed everything. My journey with my mother taught and showed me how God works in our lives. Our battles and our forgiving gave me immense opportunities to know the presence of something else in this life besides our humanness. This something else works in our favor! This something else always has our backs, so that when we trust It, miracles occur.

And what is a miracle? I define a miracle as anything that happens outside the parameters of human calculation. We ask for something, and it appears. We think positively, and it works for our benefit. We pray and are answered. The mystical is working, the nonphysical is making way, the Universal Intelligence is at work! All of it *real*. All of it *present*. All of it for us. We just need to trust.

Death and dying have been amazingly generous teachers for me. When I was four, we moved into a brand-new home my parents had built. There, I met my childhood best friend, Martha. Every single day we spent time together. She came from a large Catholic family who had dinner together every night, and more babies than I ever knew was possible. Martha would share with me that when she grew up, she was going to be a nun. Her six-year-old mind was made up. I can see us on my parent's front porch discussing God and how "He" made a difference in her life. I found this intoxicating. We were little girls, having a grown-up conversation. Martha and I were inseparable until school years forced us apart, as I was in public school and she in a private Catholic school. Even though we grew apart, and my family moved away my freshman year in high school, I never forget her or our conversations. I came home from boarding school one weekend to my mother telling me Martha had died from injuries sustained from being hit by a car. We were only fourteen years old. I asked to go see her family, to visit. I asked, "What do we do?" My mother showed me. We drove to Martha's house, left a card that I did not see, with a check inside as a donation, because as my mother said, "This is what the Catholics do." I knew it was not near enough or close enough to appropriate. I was ashamed and embarrassed. I wanted so much more. We never spoke of it again.

Jump forward to the gallery/healing center. There I was, leading my first public meditation evening, for a group to meet *their* guides. And there was Martha, for me. This was the first time I had seen her in over thirty years. Tears, joy, and my exuberant heart. She was right there, it was Martha. I could touch her. I can see her now, in a white dress, patent leather buckled shoes, and white ankle socks, her bangs held back with a metal bobby pin, her brown hair bouncing, cut right to her chin, as it was when I last saw her. She was so happy. Pure joy radiated from her. I felt and still feel such gratitude for her coming to me that night. It was *so* good to be with her again, to see her so happy.

As I young girl I remember visiting with an aunt and uncle who had lost their son to a terminal illness when he was very young. When we left, I asked my mother how was it that my aunt was doing so well? My mother thought about it and said, "She is very religious; I think it is her faith." That answer made an impression on my young mind. I can still see the day, everyone involved, and my aunt's face. I noticed a polar opposite response from another couple, who as very close friends of my family were also an aunt and uncle, whose only son had also died young of a terminal illness; even from my little girl awareness, I knew they were alcoholics and suffering. Their son Tommy had been a bit older than me, and had always been so much fun and kind to me. These experiences with the deaths of my only two male cousins gave me the gift of this awareness of how people moved on after loss and was profound for me. Faith, whatever that was, made a difference.

Tommy had been a sailor, always in a sailboat, having grown up on Cape Cod. I was nearly age twelve when I saw him again. I sat in the back seat of the car as my parents were driving us to Marblehead, Massachusetts to visit relatives. I looked out my window as we came upon an expanse of land, and instantly no less than a hundred "dead" people appeared, with Tommy in the center of them. He looked right at me and waved. This mass of people crossed the street in front of my father's car, and Tommy continued to look right at me. He was in the same sailing clothes I have a photo of him in, his blonde hair falling over his eyes. He starred at me, and let me know all was well, and that he was still sailing. I was pretty quiet for the rest of that day.

———————————

Why me? Why do some of us see spirit and others do not? I believe that our loved ones are always trying to connect with us. I have seen this over and over again, but unless you are open to this belief or if you have to have contact made in a specific manner, you may miss it. When you have resistance, your loved ones cannot make successful contact. They cannot get through. It is not easy for our transitioned loved one to learn how to do this, be it in a dream or through another human. Be open to any way they can find to be welcomed. Many people are in fear, anger, and inconsolable grief around a loved one's death, which makes it impossible for their transitioned loved one to successfully contact them. The loved one and the bereaved are on two different frequencies. A frequency of love attracts a frequency of love. When we transition, we are fully in a frequency of love.

Once I did a presentation at a local senior center about this. Afterward, one woman who was quite distraught and deeply grieving her husband's death was turning to leave the room, and I was told to hug her from the back. I did. I wrapped my arms around her, and as I did, I gently said, "Your husband told me to do this." She turned with tears in her eyes and said, "He always would hug me from the back when I was in the kitchen, it was our thing." My prayer is that this was helpful for her to know and to believe his presence still exists.

12

LET ME KNOW YOU'VE LANDED

Joy is the most infallible sign of the Presence of God.

~ *Pierre Teilhard de Chardin*

◆

My first experience with a transitioned loved one letting me know they had landed safely on the other side, or in heaven if you prefer, was unexpected. My mother's sister was dying. One morning I awoke from what I would then call a dream, but now, a sacred alternate reality experience, of being witness to my deceased grandmother coming for her daughter, my dying aunt. It began with me seeing my aunt in her hospital bed in her house. My grandmother walked into the "scene," she faced me and let me know all was well, and that it was time for her to walk her daughter home. My grandmother looked so beautiful, graceful, and light-filled as she reached for my aunt's hand. My aunt rose from her bed without issue, looking fully healthy. They both stopped, turned, and looked directly at me, as if to say, *see, this is how it is done.* Then they walked away. It was exactly like watching a play. I had never seen anything like this before. What was happening?

As I stood up from my bed a bit confused, the phone rang. My cousin was calling me to let me know our aunt had just died.

I was not on an intentional spiritual path at this time. This happened years before my gallery, before I had begun any ministerial, Reiki, or energy studies. As I have evolved, I now ask a loved one, when it is appropriate, to let me know when they have landed, to give me a sign they have arrived home. I ask for a few reasons. One is that it is fun. Secondly, it is lovely for them to know they can make a connection to someone in human form from the other side, and the assignment makes it easier for them to do so with loved ones. Think of it as being given homework. Also, many times when a person has gone through either a long-drawn-out experience or a shockingly quick death experience here from this plane, they are sent to what I am told is the Spirit Hospital. This is a place of deep rest, retreat, and healing as a person's Masters and teachers work on them before they are ready to enter the Kingdom of Heaven. I have never seen a child in the Spirit Hospital.

After several months of weekly visits to Nina's home, it was time for her to transition. Sitting with her in hospice, planning her life celebration, I had the opportunity to ask her, "Let me know you have landed." She promised.

Driving to the church for her memorial service, which I was officiating, I asked once again, "Please, Nina, give me that sign, let me know you are home." I had not heard from her yet. Within a half-mile I had to stop for a gaggle of ducks crossing the road coming from my right. I thought to myself, I had driven this road hundreds of times and never seen ducks on it. My curious mind noted I was far away from a body of water. Watching the ducks cross the road to my left, I looked up, and I saw it. The road sign at the intersection said **Nina Drive.** I cannot count the times I had gone by this intersection and never had I ever noticed that well-worn street sign before. Thank you, Nina.

My sister-in-law had been brought up on her still-active family farm in Ohio. Several generations later, it is still being farmed by her relatives. A few days after she transitioned from a year-long relationship with cancer, I stood at my kitchen sink asking, "Sara, let me know you have landed. Remember those conversations we had? You said if you could, you would?"

And I went about my day. I decided to go to my favorite farm stand to gather freshly dug potatoes for dinner. In the photo, you can see the first one I chose from the pile! My hand went right to it. When I lifted it out and up from the bushel of taters, my smile must have lit up the room. What I love the most about this is that Sara was all heart, yet one would not call her demonstrative. During her dance with cancer, she told me she loved me every time I left her. She kissed me. To me, she made up for years of not expressing—and then, this gift of the perfect message. (No, I did not cook it. I placed it on my kitchen window ledge, above the sink, and gazed at it for days.)

One of my God sisters, Miranda—a healer, actress, artist, voice extraordinaire, Medicine Woman, and Star Being—transitioned as of this writing, exactly one year ago today on August 28, 2019. It was my privilege, honor, and love to be with her the entire day before she transitioned. How fitting that I am completing my unscheduled writing with her "let me know you've landed" message on this anniversary. (There are no coincidences.)

Miranda loved spider medicine. She also was the only friend I have had who owned a pet snake, living in her home, free to slither anywhere. No, not a small one. Oh yes, and a cat. Back to Spider Medicine. This is the oldest Native American medicine known. The spider represents the four directions, plus the four winds of change, in the total of its eight legs. It also represents infinite creativity. If you knew Miranda it was easy to understand why the spider was one of her most cherished medicines. We originally met when she came to the door of my healing center selling rattles made by her potter husband, complete with her original designs, from the trunk of her car. It was love at first sight.

The day after she transitioned, I went to our back-porch door to go outside to greet the day with my morning coffee. I did not get too far, for an enormous spider, and I use the word "enormous" with emphasis, and its gigantic web filled the upper third of the doorway. I had never before been in the presence of such a large spider. This web, at thirty-one inches wide, spanned the distance from door jamb to door jamb and was at least fifteen inches in depth. My face would have been covered if I had walked through it to the outside. Yes, I stood in awe, laughing with Miranda. I left it there for a while and went out the front door instead. Later that day I gently removed the web. This continued for two more mornings. Each morning another *huge* web and large spider were blocking the entrance of our back-porch door. On the third morning, Miranda and I had a chat. I asked her to please find another way to communicate with me. *I am glad to know you've landed, but enough with the spiders.* It worked. This had never happened before, and it has never happened since.

The day after a client transitioned, I was outside in our yard, asking her to let me know when she had landed. The same afternoon of my request, a chipmunk sat on top of the Buddha's head sculpture by our back door. My deceased friend had loved this Buddha. She commented on it whenever I brought her over for a visit. The chipmunk sat there for over half an hour. I asked if it was my friend. It would turn to look at me, then turn back into position, and not moving otherwise, continue to sit. I would walk by it and it simply sat. Never had a chipmunk ever sat on any garden fixture we have. Never has one sat since.

13

SOUL-TO-SOUL COMMUNICATION

Escape from the black cloud that surrounds you.
Then you will see your own light as radiant as the full moon.

~ Rumi

◆

My belief, knowing, and experience show me that we are souls residing in physical bodies. Our True Identity, that which does all the living, resides within this human instrument, vessel, container. You may call it the spirit. Spirit, not born of an earthly birth, communes differently than by using outer human verbiage. When one has developed a heightened awareness of senses, communication happens through time and space, not only on the linear earth plane through various verbal expressions. Mainstream terminology may call it mediumship or having psychic abilities. My view is, it is pure soul-to-soul dialogue, having nonphysical conversations. I believe we each have an innate ability to commune nonverbally. Is this not what feelings are doing? When we empathize with another, we are expressing our feelings to them. When we sense another person is sad, or happy, or ill, this is partial communication in picking up on their sense of self. When we wordlessly hug another person with an intention that they will feel better, this is nonverbal communication. To those who have practiced and are open enough, the experience of realizing we can hear or speak with another being through what the human mind sees as thought or energy is simply another way of correspondence.

Why does this not happen for everyone? I believe that soul-to-soul communicating is not a skill, but an effect of faith and understanding of Universal Law. Yes, it may take practice, and yes, there are people more adept at this than others. My years of study—with Unity, Science of Mind, *A Course in Miracles,* and reading, reading, reading—have all helped me to develop my beliefs and therefore how I see this life and its infinite potential. People unconsciously place resistance on their path through fearful talk, judgment, or labeling anything bad, not good, unusual, or weird. If your belief is *that hearing from loved ones who have transitioned or being able to commune with one who is too ill to talk is impossible,* this is resistance. We are of one mind. (These transmissions can be had with anything, for God Source is in all things. One can ask a question or feel its beingness and intuit an answer.)

Soul-to-soul communication can be extremely useful when a person is transitioning and in a resistant state of not letting go. Fear is always the seed that any resistance stems from. I do not have to be physically near a person to support them through soul-to-soul communication. I can be miles away, in another state. Distance is almost better, for in my experience, there is less human ego involved, which creates easier access.

———

Laine was a young woman whose mother, Martha, had been a client of mine. I was very involved in Martha's transition, supporting the family and officiating the memorial celebration. Laine was in her late twenties. Her mother had been ill her daughter's entire life. Laine's father, who I had never met, was distant, living on the island of Tahiti with his new wife. Laine's stepfather was a gem. Since her mothers' transition, Laine and I had grown very close. She was, for many years, the daughter I never had, looking to me for support, advice, and sharing great joys.

In the early hours of a December morning, Laine's mother Martha, having died two and a half years earlier, came to me during my sleep, jolting me awake with this statement: "Deborah, get up, Laine needs you, please." Once again in awe of life's possibilities, I rose from the bed. Instantly my phone rang. It was Laine. Her father had drowned in a flash flood on the island of Tahiti.

A regular client came to me for support, as her best friend from high school had died. They had become adults with separate lives, yet her obvious love for him was palpable during our session. This easily allowed for his presence to be known to me in a clairsentient manner. She was deeply concerned for his young family and his sister. The session went well, ending with her feeling greater peace concerning her friend's transition.

That evening I sat in our living room reflecting on my day, when directly across from me, sat my client's deceased friend. Surprise! But that was not the most interesting part. The most intriguing thing was the bouncing, very happy, extremely joyful light being playing in our living room. I saw that it was a dog. I instantly knew it was his dog. A dog had not been mentioned in our session. I had seen our own pets in Spirit in our homes many times, but never another person's animal.

My client's friend told me to call her and let her know he had been here and to be sure to tell her about the dog, that she needs to know. *Okay, I will,* I promised. He left.

Even though it was late, he had been adamant, so I texted my client and asked if she could talk. She called me immediately. I felt a bit awkward, talking about a dog who was running joyfully around my living room in spirit, but I did. I had promised her friend I would. I told her about his visitation, how happy and peaceful he was, and then about the dog. Did she know if he had any pets?

After the tears and the "oh my Gods" quieted, my client shared that her friend's dog had died the day after he had. His wife had them buried together in one casket. This was not public knowledge. This information received via her friend allowed her to feel more secure of his eternal spirit; that when we die, we are not gone, we are only gone from this plane of existence to another. I hope that this information also helped his family to find a sense of peace during their time of grief.

My husband's dear friend, Jim, was in hospice, having a difficult time transitioning. In my perception, he had lived a life of being very controlling. He had been a respected member of the mainstream medical community. He and I shared a mutual respect for one another, as we had long ago acknowledged our views on attaining healthy well-being were extremely different.

We drove two hours to the hospice so Bill, as one member of Jim's closest clan of males, could extend support and say goodbye. I accompanied my husband because I love hospices, and also to back him up because he is not as comfortable with death as I am. Plus, I was told to. Spirit had told me I was to be there for Jim's girlfriend—although I had only met her twice before.

Waiting in the hospice's living room area, I was guided to not go into Jim's room. We did not have a friendship, yet we both loved the same man. I sat and trusted my inner directives. Jim's girlfriend entered. She was very glad I was there. Immediately she brought the conversation around to what did I do for work, *exactly?* As I shared, she opened up about how hard Jim's dying experience had been thus far. With her permission, I offered to do whatever I could to help. I let it go at that.

The day after our hospice visit, Jim's soul reached out to me. I had spontaneous communication with him, as he was struggling to let go, trying to control what he saw as a finite process. Often in these situations of a personality who is grounded in a 3D mentality, I offer a literal explanation of what is happening to them, which traditionally has been very helpful. I explained how we are not our body, that the soul, the essence of yourself is eternal, that you continue thriving, just in a different reality. Your soul is simply disconnecting from your ego body. You will continue to thrive on another plane of existence. Look for your loved one's hands coming through the veil, look for them, follow them.

The following morning, Jim's girlfriend texted me and asked if there was anything I could do, because "it is really bad." I went into my space of communicating with Jim, explaining that he needed to look for his mother's hands through the veil. I stayed with him, guiding, talking, for maybe ten minutes. A few moments later my phone pinged. The text said, "Thank you, he is gone."

14

BRITT

*Being deeply loved by someone gives you strength
while loving someone deeply gives you courage.*

~ *Lao Tzu*

◆

The above quote defines Britt to a tee. The courage she showed each time I saw her overshadowed any fears. Britt loved her husband and two boys immensely. The strength she exemplified during her dance with cancer was beyond anything I had ever witnessed. The word I would use is *composure.* She preferred the small versions of Ritz and Saltines so no cracker crumbs would get on the furniture, at her home or mine. I stocked my shelves.

This sharing is about courage, strength, composure, Britt letting me know she had landed, death and dying, as well as soul-to-soul communication. All of it. I am honored to have known this soul. Oh, and she loved chocolate.

By the time Britt came to me as a client, she had been living with a rare cancer for several years. Metaphysical or spiritual notions, or anything other than mainstream curing was unfamiliar to her. Physically and intelligently, Britt was working very, very hard at surviving. She was a well-educated, mind-oriented person; my most challenging type of client. Why? Because people like Britt want to fix something, figure out what to do, or find a linear answer, rather than open their hearts and seek from within. She came to me angry that after many years her husband had finally made it to the top of his industry, making the money that afforded them more linear freedom, and now, due to her cancer, they could not travel. Britt was so encased in doing the right thing, living life a certain way, that her intellect had gotten the better of her. Joy was not resonant from Britt—only seeking a way through this experience via fighting for, at, and about cancer. I found Britt to be fighting so hard that she was not embracing life, but hanging by raw fingertips.

I treaded lightly during our first session. This profound work can be a lot to allow in, plus this way of perceiving was entirely new to her. I looked for an opening, a small, slight way the Light could enter her practiced thinking, a way my words could land within her. I waited for a door that is not quite shut tight, with a crack so slight I could lovingly pry it open. Silently I asked God to help me see an opportunity.

At this point in her journey, Britt shared that she went to the hospital several days a week for transfusions. This was a way to extend her life that she and her husband both agreed upon. She went on to share that each week they took blood, and gave her the same lab result news over and over. It was not hopeful. *Ah, my opening.*

I asked if she ever thought, at this point, to ask her doctor to only share with her when there were positive improvements, rather than keep reporting the poor lab results. "No, we had not."

Considering this took a deep thought process for Britt. So many people forget that this is their body and they get to choose what they want for treatment. I tell every client who comes to me who is also a medical patient that you get to say, "No thank you" to your doctor. It is your body, your life. You get to choose. The most important aspect of your choices is that you believe in them. I encourage my clients to make choices based on what they feel good about and have faith in, not a decision based on fear. If you believe in radiation, do it. If you believe in chemotherapy, do it. Only take action on a choice you are aligned with. Do not say yes to anything you do not believe in, because *then you are simply at war with yourself, as well as not being in full receptivity of your choice.*

The following week Britt sat down and told me right away that she had told her doctor to please not tell them any of the lab findings unless they improve. She told the doctor that she and her husband understood the stakes here, but being told over and over again, hearing those negative words, was too heavy. Ah, Britt was feeling empowered. It was obvious to me; she was lighter when she spoke, she was less resistant, and she was greatly relieved.

"How does that feel to you? To ask your doctor?"

"It felt really good."

She went on to chat about the landscapers making too much noise in her yard too early that morning. I asked, "do you ever just sit outside and enjoy your beautiful yard?"

"No."

"You may want to try that. Do you ever just go up to your room and take nap, a quiet rest?"

"No."

Mind you, both simple "noes" came after some deep thought and with contorted facial expressions that demonstrated an *inner acknowledgment of "why have I not done that before?"*

One day, Britt came to her session in a zebra-print top. I complimented her on it. She explained, "Oh, it is my kind of cancer—it is a rare case, so they call it a zebra." I had never heard this term before, but I was more aghast that she wore a shirt that every moment reminded her of her cancer. So much for the compliment. Every time she opened her drawer, every time she looked in the mirror, did the laundry, hung this jersey up, she saw her cancer—the very rare one that the medical world saw no hope for. The rare zebra. In the world of energy medicine, we want to redirect to joyful feelings, or at the least, to a hopeful perspective. I doubt she felt joy when she looked at her shirt. Or even hope.

At the next session, Britt casually mentioned she had sat in her yard that past week. She also had gone upstairs to her bedroom in the middle of the day to rest. Both were new and enjoyable experiences for her. Imagine being in your fifties and the idea of making time for yourself is a new concept. I began to see the minutest flashes of joy in our sessions. A smile. A glint in her eye. Britt came weekly. I asked if it was okay for me to hug her goodbye. She said yes. She was stiff. It was uncomfortable. There was no response. Many times, Britt had someone drive her to our sessions and this allowed me to meet her sisters and friends. Britt was doing an amazing job of living her life as a wife and mother of two grown sons and someone who loved to host gatherings. Yet, joy was not front and center, and it seemed it was often difficult for her to find the energy of ease at all.

Britt's rigidness pushed me to be better at what I did. Her results from the energy work were significant. Pain left her body, nausea stopped, headaches went away; yet I wanted to support her to soften, to guide her to feel some joy during her days. Once I asked her if she could think it possible that somewhere in the universe there was a way for her body to heal and cancer to be gone. She could not get there. Okay. Joy was my goal. She had such a wonderful smile, I wanted her to feel a reason to use it more. I just never saw what I thought was enough joy from her. It was obvious to me that joy wanted to be expressed. In my very human-ego thinking, I thought I had failed her, even though she kept coming for appointments. I had to trust in the fact she kept coming back, feeling a positive something in her life that she wanted more of. I had a difficult time sensing improvement from her. I had to remind myself that Britt's healing was between her and God.

One morning Britt missed her appointment. Historically, she was always thoughtful about letting me know if she would not be able to make it, even texting from a hospital bed. I texted her phone to check in. No response. She had just been to see me the week before. I sat down and checked in with Spirit; Britt had made her transition. I asked Britt to let me know when she had landed and was fully on the other side. She immediately told me to not forget the zebras. Again, we chatted about the shirt! I laughed.

Shortly after this, I received a text from her husband, whom I had never met, letting me know Britt had made her transition the night before. Letting her go was the hardest thing he had ever done. Britt's husband shared that she had asked him, please, no more measures to draw this out, her battle had gone on long enough. I was so grateful she had found her voice. He said he would let me know about the arrangements.

I went into our television room to ground myself with a silly show. I clicked on a sitcom I had never watched before. Why? I had absolutely no idea. It took place in a hospital setting. At the very moment I tuned in, the intern was reporting to the head physician about a common pneumonia case and he came out of his office ranting, "Why can't we ever get a zebra!" I was once again in awe of life, deeply grateful and laughing at Britt's fabulous humor.

That afternoon I went to visit a nursing home/hospice to see a friend who works there. After we had our chat time, she wanted me to visit a particular nursing home resident because she was simply so wonderful. As we got off the elevator, we could see her clearly, sitting in her wheelchair. She was deeply engrossed with an orange crayon on paper. As we approached her chair, she looked up and said to me, "Look, a zebra." Yes, she was coloring a zebra. My friend, standing behind the patient's wheelchair, had just heard about my morning story and all she could do was laugh and mouth, *"It's a zebra!"*

A Catholic Mass and celebration of Britt's life was being held at a sweet stone church perfectly situated on an idyllic small hill. I had always wanted to go inside. Since I had no connection with the family as clergy, this was the very first client whose life celebration I was not officiating as the minister. It felt very odd to me to be entering the church as a congregant, and not having spoken personally with the family to help plan this ritual. I had taken only a few steps inside the church when Britt's fabulous sister tackled me like a football player. Grasping my arms with each hand, and looking directly in my eyes with words of profound gratitude, she spoke of how I had given her sister permission to seek *joy* in her life. Britt's sister was quite determined to get me to own this and her appreciation was palpable. She went on and on, talking about Britt being joyful from our work together, all the while not letting go of her hold on me.

We hugged, teared up, and I took this great gift with me as I found a pew to sit in. Britt's husband spoke the eulogy and I was quite taken with his stories of their honeymoon through Europe, and how Britt loved the huge pretzels and just had to have them. You could feel her smile as he spoke. Ah, the joy of Britt. At the end of this most eloquent eulogy, her husband thanked Britt's Reiki Minister for all she did for her.

I share this because it was and is deeply important to me that the work I do is of positive benefit. There was a part of me that felt I had failed Britt, and without these beautiful words and conveyances I may have carried that belief with me—and thankfully, for I have no idea what that would have done to me. I am so very grateful I was told otherwise.

Thank you, Britt, for allowing me the privilege of knowing you, witnessing you, and being part of your journey.

15

REQUESTING AND RECEIVING

You are either attracting or repelling
according to your mental attitudes.

~ *Dr. Ernest Holmes*

◆

My new friend Emily and I would meet in the early mornings to converse as I walked my dog. To this day I refer to Emily as one of my God sisters. I am blessed to know amazing women. Women who are talented, faithful, strong, funny, smart, beautiful, tender, courageous, and vulnerable. In my life now and days gone by, these God sisters of mine hold a deeply sacred connection in my heart-knowing. Not seeing one another for months or years at a time, even having let go of our human friendships, does not lessen the role they have played in my life. Our combined faith and practices have supported each other at various times along our spiritual paths. We are most certainly united through our love of the Divine, no matter what personal label we have for it.

At this time in my journey, I found Emily extraordinary. She had been a brilliant computer coder, and now due to physical issues, she was living on disability. Emily, a focused spiritual practitioner for many years, had once been around the world, traveling extensively. At the time we initially connected, her awareness was far beyond mine. She had a sexual abuse history which she eventually allowed forgiveness to carry. Emily had years of study, living, and being *A Course in Miracles* student, as well as an Amma devotee. (For more about Amma, please visit Amma.org.)

We talked for hours. Emily's perception and understanding drew from me a curiosity I did not know I had, as well as knowledge and awareness that had not yet been revealed. She spoke of the universe in language that was foreign to me, yet intensely familiar. One day I nonchalantly stated, "I wish I could see this eternal universe you speak of." She replied, "Just ask." So, I did.

That night before I closed my eyes to sleep, I requested to see the universe, this eternalness. Anything I state in sharing this experience will not do the actual occurrence justice. Any words or description will rightly fall short. I found myself dreaming, in an alternate dimension, watching, as I was "amid" darkness. There was an extremely slow, consistent spiral-like turning to this vast space. There were no edges, no beginning or end. It appeared boundless. There was nothing outside of it. There were thousands of little white dots. I was telepathically told each white dot was a universe. (Gasp!) Our universe was pointed out to me. I was in awe. Not only because I had simply asked and here it was, but here it was! Even now, remembering, I can feel my ecstasy of this revelation.

No, no one was talking to me, like we humans do. I call much of my knowing "downloads." In receiving multidimensional, non-earth communications, there is a use of other senses applied to hear and/or attain understanding. Some call this intuition, while others name it a feeling, gut instinct, an inner voice, the upper room, mediumship, or psychic ability. Perhaps it is simply acute listening skills that transcend time and space.

We had lived in our new home for a few months. I was settled and a bit bored. Spirit kept telling me, do not advertise, do not put up a sign. I desperately wanted an outdoor sign. It was all designed. Despite my enthusiasm, the guidance was always *no*. We had purchased a home on a main road with the intention that I would use signage to advertise my practice. How could I let others know I was here, in this new town, this new area? It was clear, though, that I was not to make known my healing practice, yet. "Yet" was the operative message for me.

In frustration and boredom, one day I gave it all to God. I am familiar with the energy I held as I spoke out loud to the powers that be. "God, if I cannot put out a sign and begin my practice here, I want the perfect part-time job. I want to use all my skills, have a job close to home and allow myself to get to know this area better. Thank you." That was it, clear and simple. Then I went on with my day.

The very next day (yes, the very next day), I received a call from Susan, the former lead nurse at the farm where I had been caretaker. Susan owned a nursing agency. Her firm had just taken on a new client, an elderly couple who just "happened" to live the next town over from me. Mind you, we now lived more than an hour and a half away from Susan's agency. It made no earthly sense to me, that she would have a client in this area. I came to learn that the couple's daughter lived in the same location as the nursing agency. Since the agency's well-known, upscale boutique caregiving reputation preceded them, the family hired this organization.

The owner wanted me to consider a general caretaking role. No, I am not a nurse. I have geriatric care management experience and hospice care training that combined with my other skills to make her feel this way: "We do not know yet what we need, but I trust you and you can let us know what you think is required. Plus, you live near them. I know no one else in that area. It is a beautiful private home that requires overseeing. Like the farm, you will probably fit right in. The couple is refusing care. She is in the early stages of Alzheimer's and her husband recently had a stroke. How about you drive by, think about it, and call me back tomorrow."

Not a surprise to me, in investigating our new surroundings since we had moved, their home was on the only side road I had driven down. I enjoyed the road so much when I had originally discovered it, that I went back a few times to enjoy the houses and scenery. On one of my drives, I had already noticed the old carved sign at the end of the potential new client's driveway, reminding me of the carved sign at the end of the farm's driveway. I drove by as promised. The landscape crew was working close to the road, reminding me of the farm landscaper in my previous position. One could not see the house from the road. Same as the farm. Remember, there are no coincidences.

I was in awe of God once again. I had *just* asked for the perfect part-time job—the day before! I called the agency owner back and I agreed to meet with the family, to gain insight into the couple and their needs. Personally, how could I say no? This is what answered prayer is all about. I had worked alongside this agency owner for two years, but two years ago. I had just asked for a perfect part-time job for me. And this agency, over an hour and a half from our area, just said yes to clients not in their district, ten minutes from my new home. Really?

Was it the perfect job you ask? Did it use all my gifts? Yes, indeed. More than I ever could have imagined possible. The wife, Marsha, was direct and intelligent. From the moment we met, we got along famously. I had worked on an Alzheimer's unit in my nursing home days, as well as cared for my mother-in-law when she lived with Alzheimer's. The entire energy of the position was very familiar. Marsha loved to do errands, still driving in her car. As her disease progressed, I took over the driving, and this taught me my way around our new area. They had a large home with all that I was used to from my previous position: housekeeper, gardeners, landscapers. Marsha and I grew close. She often said God had sent me to her. Even as her memory darkened, her words still expressed appreciation. This acknowledgment was mutual.

The husband, Nathaniel, was a curmudgeon. Stubborn and downright difficult. He expected everything to keep going as it always had and he expected his wife to keep waiting on him hand and foot. He did not want me there and made that explicitly clear. He no longer drove and struggled with walking. I made a deal with him: I would try it out for three months, and if after that time, he wanted me to leave his employ, I would. I felt confident I was meant to be there. After applying my deepest amount of patience and faith, I earned Nathaniel's respect to the point that he allowed me to give his face the weekly shave.

The similarities and connections between our lives kept revealing themselves. Marsha's birthday was the same as my mother-in-law's. She also had been a counselor, having her master's degree in Divinity. She was the daughter of a banker, as I am. Her maiden name was the same name as the name of the farm where I had previously been the caretaker. Nathaniel's birthday was the day before my father's, and earlier in his life, he had played golf in Florida with a college acquaintance of mine. My favorite "coincidence" was the day a Christmas card arrived in their mail. It was a holiday family photo card from an old friend of Marsha's. She had spoken of her friend over and over again to me, as they had shared a memorable time as young women which was embedded in her long-term memory. I did not recognize the family name on the holiday card, but the photo looked so familiar. In a flash, there it was! My closest girlfriend's brother and his wife! I recognized them from their wedding photos. Marsha's lifelong friend was my friend's brother's mother-in-law. Wow!

This job was not always easy, nor was it a smooth experience. In all the love that I felt for this couple, their family dynamics and history were filled with pain, abuse, and what appeared to me as challenges. And yet, yes, I stayed. Somehow, I believed I was making a difference for them as individuals. I strongly felt I was offering unconditional love, filling a vacancy that neither one of them had experienced as children. The family dynamics were especially challenging for me, and other staff and I met in disagreements, but

I stayed in faith until otherwise directed. I never had any doubt that I was meant to be there with this couple. They felt the same. I cherish my time with them, fully believing it was a sacred contract we had agreed upon before this incarnation.

I spent a jam-packed year and a half in their employ and as their confidant. I left in the springtime, the day before my birthday. I loved this couple, but Spirit made it clear my time with them was complete. It was time for me to renew my private healing practice. It took deep prayer for me to leave. I struggled. My faith told me I had completed what I had come here to achieve. The only way I could give my notice was to trust my inner compass, even if I did not fully understand why.

Immediately, my husband and I went away to the Maine coast for a few days so I could decompress and process. The day after we came back, I became very ill. I am rarely sick. I felt miserable and slept for ten days. Finally, at my husband's prodding, I went to the doctor. Nothing medical was found. This obvious healing journey left me as quickly as it had come. One day I woke up and felt renewed. I knew this illness was a drastic clearing of all the negativity I had been exposed to during this caregiving experience. I knew I was being taken care of, what Spirit called "reestablished."

From that point, the flow into my full-time practice was incredibly easy. Funny, I was plenty busy even without any advertising. Grace fills all cracks.

On September 8 of that same year (five months after I left the couple's employ), I was exhausted all day. It was the anniversary of my father's death, but my intuition said my exhaustion was not due to that. I went to bed in the midafternoon to rest, asking Spirit, *what should I do? Are you calling me to do distance work?* Recently there had been raging fires and floods throughout the world. Often, I am called to do planetary grid work (or planetary healing work), so I did. I was still exhausted. There was a palpable sense of disturbance I could not put my finger on. I tossed and turned for hours. I finally dozed off. Marsha's voice awoke me from a deep sleep right before midnight. "Go to Facebook, Deborah."

"Why am I hearing your voice?" I asked.

"Go, go now."

I did just that. The top post on my Facebook page was about a home invasion in a neighboring town. I immediately knew. I stayed awake reading anything I could. Nathaniel and Marsha had died, as well as others who were in their home. Due to Spirit guiding me to leave their employ, there was no chance I would have been present during the event. Remember also, my father had died on September eighth. And my mother's first marriage was on September eighth.

Two mornings after her death, my friend's voice woke me a second time. "Deborah, you were right. Go to Facebook."

There on the top of my feed was a photograph of many different dogs, looking up, with the saying, "This is what greets you in heaven."

Marsha and Nathaniel had loved many dogs during their marriage. In discussing death with her, I once promised Marsha that all the dogs she had loved would meet her when she died and crossed to the other side. She missed them very much. How fun of her to let me know. I have not seen the dog post on Facebook since, nor was it there later that day when I looked for it on my page. Remaining open, love can message us through all of time and space.

I do not believe in coincidences. I realize this sounds silly to many people, but in connecting the dots in our lives, we can see, with clarity, the road signs God gave us. I believe our life is a cosmic web. A web created of points of light which represent all our connections from previous lives, sacred contracts, present life energy, and what we are creating currently. When we choose to listen deeply, to trust whatever our language is for the Divine, we are enormously blessed with awarenesses otherwise unknowingly understood from an earthly perspective.

16

MEDICAL MIRACLES

You are not here to bring Light into the world.
You're here to be Light.

~ Abraham-Hicks

◆

My faithful understanding that all is possible has shown me miracles. Sometimes they are only for me to see, sometimes a client recognizes them also, and sometimes I am praying for another and even though they do not acknowledge the shift as a miracle (God intervening), I do.

It is one of my strongest beliefs that a Universal Creator Presence, no matter what you call it, is here to correspond to our thinking and to aid us when we are in distress.

My first hospital experience with a client, Karin, was the result of an energy healing session. When I scanned her body, which is not done by touching, but with hands held a few inches above the physical body, I felt something in the area of her right breast, the energy of heat and explosion. It was unfamiliar to me. When she rose and we discussed her session, she smiled. "Oh, my implant must have burst."

In a follow-up visit with her physician, he confirmed that the implant had indeed burst. Without hesitation, Karin chose to have her right breast removed. Her left breast had already been surgically removed in a previous procedure. Now, she wanted to be "in balance," she said. We continued weekly sessions until she was scheduled to have the operation. Her surgeon very kindly allowed my presence in pre-op. I met Karin and her husband at the hospital early in the day. Karin wanted me with her, right beside her. As we waited in reception for her name to be called, my hand laid on her back and I allowed energy to flow.

Karin's name was called for registration, so we walked to a desk attended by a nurse. To me, Karin was drunk with Reiki. The nurse, however, immediately accused me of giving the patient drugs and called the surgeon to confirm my privileges. Karin and I never forgot that nurse's shining statement to us. As the patient at the next registration desk was crying, expressing concern and fright about her surgery, the nurse looked at us and said, "See, that is how the patient should be."

After registration, where Karin could barely sign her name, we were brought into pre-op. As Karin lay in her bed, totally relaxed, a nurse came over to mainline her with a sedative. She said to us, "It is obvious she is very relaxed and does not need this, but it is protocol." Karin smiled. After a while, the nurse came back and asked me what I was doing. Did I do aromatherapy, is that what was helping this patient? We chatted.

As they took Karin into surgery, I waited with her husband. A very staunch man, not much for expressing emotions, he did state he was grateful to me, for he believed he could be no help at all in such a situation. We were told it would take two to three hours for the surgery, which would remove the implant as well as the remaining breast tissues. After just forty-five minutes, the surgeon appeared to speak with us. She was highly impressed with the grace and ease of the surgery. She predicted it would take two weeks for Karen's range of motion to begin to come back and assured us that Karin would be kept pain-free during the night. I left for home.

I heard from Karin a few days later. She wanted me to know she had experienced no pain, at all. She wanted me to know she had refused all pain medications at the hospital, clearly stating she had no pain. Karin was upset, for she got hold of her chart and it read, "patient refuses pain meds," *not* "patient reports lack of pain."

A journalist who was a regular at my healing center at this time met with Karin. An article was in the works about Karin's surgery experience, and the journalist wanted to interview the doctor as well. We found this very exciting. Such an article could give other people hope for a smooth surgical experience. (Reiki practitioners were not then a regular option in hospitals as they are today.) Unfortunately, the surgeon refused to speak with the journalist. Yet, we were grateful she had allowed my presence in the hospital at all.

Karin had a 90% range of motion by the end of the first post-surgery week. She never took even an aspirin for pain relief. Please know that Karin was a lifelong yoga student and had been seeing me weekly for a few months. Her faith-filled devotion and positive attitude were her best tools for such a favorable experience.

A phone call from Carole, a forty-something recently divorced woman I did not know. resulted in a meet-and-greet home visit a week before her upcoming colon cancer surgery. Since we had no time to work together before the surgery as I had with Karin, I explained what I could offer her and Carole requested I be with her the day of her surgery, in pre-op and through to post-op.

As I sat with her in pre-op, we were told Carole's doctor had not yet decided if I could go any further. Carole had requested that I be with her in the operating room to offer her relaxing words before they put her under anesthesia. This experience would support her to feel fully aligned in love, much like I do when leading meditations. In pre-op, Carole was fully relaxed. A nurse kept a cautious eye out on us (particularly me) as she went in and out of the space. As Carole listened to my voice, I saw an angel and heard the words: "They are letting you in." Next, in came a nurse, handing me an all-white cover-up. She said, "We are letting you into the surgery. Put this on, I will be back in a moment to get you both." I had never been with a client in the operating room before. This was very exciting.

When we entered the room, I was formally welcomed and individually introduced to the surgical team. It was amazing how respectful and welcoming they were of my presence. They sat me at Carole's head. As I guided her into relaxation, she was prepared for surgery. The nurse who we had met in pre-op guided me out before the surgery began. She asked me to follow her. She brought me to the nurse's locker room, opened her locker, and handed me a book on prayer. She said, "I read this at the beginning of every shift. The surgeon was really glad you were here, they believe in everything you did. So do I." And then, blissfully blown away, I took off my white outfit and went to wait.

Later, the surgeon came to get me and walked me to post-op. All had gone extremely well. I let Carole know I was there and then drove home. I received a note with a generous check the following week, with Carole stating she was feeling great and healing with ease. I never heard from her again, until many years later, on the first day I had volunteered for an Abraham-Hicks workshop in Boston. I was at one of three alphabetically assigned sign-in tables for those who had preregistered. Who should come up to my table, but Carole and her fiancé—both looking radiantly in love.

———————————

A friend who is a holistic nurse had received a call from a hospice she once worked for, asking for her to come to do Reiki on a client who was having a difficult time passing. The family was very traditional, but they were willing to welcome any help at all. My intuitive friend felt it was I who should go, not herself, and so I went.

After taking an elevator up my very first high-rise building, I entered a small apartment, with the scent of traditional Italian "gravy" wafting in the air. (My first husband was Sicilian. I know that smell.) I could hear the sauce bubbling on their stove. It was an incredible home with glass, gold, glitz, chandeliers, and mirrors everywhere. Living together with the client (a woman in her fifties) were her husband Vincenzo, her adult son Vincenzo, and her old-world Italian mother. Her son greeted me and explained that they were all emotionally exhausted. He told me that his mother had cancer throughout her body, and could be lying in bed for a month, not moving, when one morning they would find her up in the kitchen, cooking. They each had said goodbye so many times. This had been going on for two years. "Our hospice nurse said you might be able to help us."

The son led me into his mother's bedroom, which was impeccably neat, with not one wrinkle in any blanket, sheet, or pillowcase. Exemplary care. She appeared laid out for public viewing. Other than a glance to his grandmother, he offered no introduction. The grandmother sat, holding court at the end of the room, erect in a wooden chair, dressed entirely in black (high neck, lots of lace, and a black shawl), and clasping her rosary. Vincenzo shared that she sat there every day, praying for her daughter. Every single day. She spoke no English. I decided to tread lightly here, not wanting to disrespect anyone's beliefs, nor a mother's love and faith. I refrained from energetically scanning my client's body or placing my hands upon her. I simply brought a chair to my client's bedside and sat. I held her hand. (Reiki practitioners know that the energy goes where it is most needed.) At that moment I no idea what else I could physically do without causing raised eyebrows and perhaps doubt-filled fears from the client's mother.

Silently I prayed and asked for guidance. After a bit, the son Vincenzo came in to check on me. I was so glad. He stood where we could see one another. I very gently explained that sometimes I see things and asked if he was comfortable with me sharing what I was seeing. He agreed. *Okay, here goes,* I thought.

"I do not see any signs of a child in your home, but I see a little blonde boy here, he showed me his playpen. He is waiting here to help your mother cross over. Do you know who he might be?"

Vincenzo was truly amazed. The boy was his son, who had died in the living room of this apartment, in his playpen, of choking. "Oh my God, that is my son, my Vincenzo."

I assured him he was here, which he easily believed. Then, I asked if the priest had come to give last rites. I assumed this would be a required formality, but when I had checked in, the energy had not presented itself. He told me his mother was mad at the priest and had stopped going to Mass a few years before she became ill. Vincenzo told me she had made it clear, telling them: "I want no priests."

It became apparent to me that the fear coming from the grandmother and the anger the client had at her priest and the church were resistance to allowing the Light to enter. What else could we do, but pray? I asked the son if he would welcome me to pray with them, here around his mother's bed. We all held hands, including the grandmother. I spoke a prayer, uniting us in love to release their loved one into the Light, into God's arms. Unity was called for. Little Vincenzo was very happy. The energy in the room had palpably shifted. I felt now that his little hands could reach through the veils to walk his grandmother home.

I was only there for a little over an hour. One hour of my life that is part of the fabric of my heart. As the son walked me to the door, I stated, "My only hope is that this will help her surrender and give you all relief. This was a privilege, thank you for welcoming me into your home."

When I got home, I called the hospice nurse who had originally asked for the intervention. I told her if I kept notes, I would have written "she will be gone within twelve hours. I had left their home at noon."

The next morning, the hospice nurse called to thank me. The client had transitioned at exactly midnight. The family was overwhelmed with gratitude, as was I. The nurse was amazed and thankful. And, to my amazement, she has never called me again.

———————————————

A friend had referred Eileen to me. Eileen had been diagnosed with an operable but very involved brain tumor that called for complicated surgery. She lived two hours from me, so I suggested we do prayer by telephone every morning for the two weeks we had, leading to her operation. She called me every morning at 8:00 a.m. We did not talk, nor did I offer counsel, for, with her faith as a strict Catholic, she felt it was not what she wanted. After our morning hellos, I spoke a five-part prayer treatment and we said goodbye. Very orderly. Very neat.

I met Eileen and her sister at the hospital the morning of the surgery. We were advised it would take several hours, perhaps an entire day, with three different teams of physicians—ear, eye, and brain surgeons with their associates. The last vision I had of Eileen before surgery was of her being mapped out; one member of each surgical team had placed a colored maker on her face and skull denoting their territory. The ear team was first.

I leave a hospital only when Spirit directs me to do. As we were nearing midafternoon, I heard the directive, *leave now.* Her sister was gracious and we said goodbye. We agreed she would call me when the surgery was complete, no matter the hour.

I had not been home very long when my phone rang.

"Deborah, it is the strangest thing! There is no tumor."

"What? What do you mean? They saw it, right? On x-rays? On testing?"

"Yes, all that. They have a name for it, they say it is rare, but it is a thing, a tumor, but not there now. It just looked like it was. The ear team went in and it could not be found."

I gathered my breath as I smiled on the other end of the phone, feeling I was listening to a medical miracle.

"What do you think happened?" I asked Eileen's sister.

She was silent for a bit.

"I think it's a miracle. After all my sister went through, after all the preliminary testing—I believe there was a tumor, and now there is not. Thank you, Deborah, thank you."

Our faith in Spirit creates miracles in our lives. God, the Universe, Creation can make anything happen through our faith, as long as we believe it is possible. As a note, I want to add that Eileen was not so amazed. In our post-surgery conversation, she was very firm there *was* a tumor. I could not grasp her explanation. We never spoke again.

———————————

Betty and I worked together once a week for a few weeks leading up to her day of surgery. She worked in academia and had a brilliant mind. Diagnosed with a brain tumor that could cause her to lose the use of her arm and hearing on the same side of her body, these potential effects of such a challenging surgery were cautiously guaranteed. In our first meeting, we discussed the trifold pamphlet she had been given to explain how these post-surgical effects take place, warning her of these most probable difficulties. My guidance began with offering her to choose to believe that these effects of the surgery had to be hers, or not. What did she want to believe? Choice. She threw the pamphlet away. We were off to an excellent start. (Warnings of effects may very well be what the medical world sees often and feels responsible to report, and we always have a choice as to what we are going to create for ourselves.)

The morning of the surgery at a major Boston hospital, I met Betty and her family near dawn. In the waiting room, with her daughter on one side and me on the other, we poured love and Reiki all over and through Betty. This is my definition of pre-op.

There were several of us in the family waiting room. The hospital had a nurse in each surgery that would come out and update the family as the hours went by. We had time to chat, as the nurse wanted to know who was here for the patient. On what I remember was the fifth or sixth hour, the nurse came out and sat in front of me. "The surgeon is getting very tired," she said. "The tumor is very intertwined and there is a great deal of it that does not want to come out. If you can do anything to help this along, that would be wonderful." I invited Betty's daughter to go to the chapel with me.

We sat separately in the chapel. As I prayed, a massive angel showed itself in the front of the altar area. When I picked my chin up off the pew, I beckoned to her daughter that it was time to get back.

In less than half an hour, the nurse came out to tell us the surgeon was able to remove 99% of the tumor. The nurse also pulled me aside. She said the difference my presence made was obvious and she asked to interview me for the hospital paper. Although I gave her all my contact information, I never heard from her. Disappointing, yes. But I choose to know I have helped to plant a few small seeds towards encouraging the presence of Reiki in many hospitals today. (Years later, a student of mine at this same hospital was the first nurse to write "Reiki" on a patient's chart.)

Betty never lost her hearing or the use of her arm. She was walking two miles a day with her husband within two weeks of post-op. She took me out for a first-anniversary dinner a year later. Betty and her husband have since happily and healthfully retired to Florida.

The ways God finds to arrange for our prayers to come true can be astonishing. Seriously, usually, only in hindsight can we see the story with clarity.

One weekend my husband's family was having a party for his uncle, now the family patriarch, to be presented with a gift from the Quilt of Valor Foundation to honor his years of service. Volunteers make the quilts. In this case, his daughter-in-law who is a quilter made some of it, and then I understood that the volunteer who would present it, finished it. The volunteer *happened* to live in our town. I was unsure if I was going to the party or not, as it felt like an intimate gathering for blood relatives only, but Spirit told me to go, so I did.

After the presentation of the quilt, the volunteer approached me to chat, having been told I lived near her. Our conversation started with that we had recently moved to town and then she asked what I did. As I explained my ministry, all she could say was, "You have to meet my sister Leslie and her husband, they live in town too." I gave her my card and she left.

Craig and Leslie arrived at our home the following Sunday. As they sat together on the couch, I invited them to share their story. Leslie had cried each day for the past year. She and Craig had dated when they were younger, but they broke up and went their separate ways. Both got married and divorced, then they had found one another again and married. It was obvious they were deeply in love, both faithful adults, and so very sad, as Craig had been diagnosed with a dreadful cancer and given a grim prognosis. Each day, Leslie said she would hear his voice or see him across a room and cry. She admitted she was a mess. They were not sure why they came to me, but they were desperate for help.

This was a very different session for me. First off, it was my first session with anyone living locally, since we had just moved. It felt like my coming-out party. This is a very traditional New England town and there is little traditional about me. I am always one-on-one with a client, but this couple was in this together, and God had told me to "listen to them both." I still can envision them sitting across from me as they respectfully gave each other time to speak, looking into one another's faces, holding hands, and apologizing for tears. I listened to their story, mostly to Craig's. Each time they told me what they declared as despondent fact from the medical world, and what they had seen in their own lives, I would gently state, "Or not," "Maybe," or "If you think so." I remember it felt like an echo to me, as I made these statements without any attachment; these were quiet, light comments. Usually, I am more direct, louder, and perhaps even forceful when I want to make a point. There was none of that this time. This went on for more than an hour. After they took a breath, I explained to them my God beliefs, for they were both religious and I want to always be clear with others where I am coming from so they can make a clear choice if I am who they want. I explained what I do and how I do it. I spoke with them about what I was feeling about their situation and his diagnosis, asking questions, and stating what I saw, which, based on their responses, held truth for them. Before leaving our two-hour meeting, Craig made his first of many weekly healing appointments with me.

Leslie called me a few days later to let me know that the day after our meeting was the first day in over a year that she had not cried. Their family joke quickly became that anyone making a rigid statement about anything or a "the doctor said this or that" would hear the reply "Or not." They had finally felt hope.

I believe that Craig came to me for five months or so. My memory is that he continued taking one medication during our time together. On the morning of the first scan following our work together, I received a text: "Cancer cannot be found. I am SO glad I know you!"

Craig has been cancer-free since then. How? In a nutshell (for this truly is their story to tell), we spoke of joy and perceptions, did hands-on healing and, in one memorable session, we both felt Jesus was in the room. Yet, it all came down to our goodbyes. At the time of this writing, Craig and Leslie have recently moved away, but before that day I invited them to come to sit with me, in our living room, where it all began—one last time. (It was a COVID-19 hug-free day, which we promised to make up for in the future.) We all teared up, we laughed and we loved that morning. But, Leslie's deeply focused final words will stay with me forever: "Deborah, you changed our lives."

When we say God works in mysterious ways, oh my! The week after I wrote the above story, with the phrase *"for this truly is their story to tell,"* the following testimony arrived in my email.

This is Craig Graham's story.

> I first met Rev. Deb in May 2017 right after completing my last cycle of chemotherapy for advanced metastatic prostate cancer. The first meeting was intended for my wife to find a counselor in dealing with my grim diagnosis by the doctors.
>
> We sat on her couch for nearly two hours answering questions and giving a history of what brought us to her. My wife (Leslie) and I confidently told her that the medical treatment was going to reduce cancer but, according to my oncologist, it would eventually return. Rev. Deb sat in her chair with bright eyes and a sage-like grin; she stated firmly, "Or not." There were many of these "or nots" scattered throughout the session and

later we would quietly chuckle when these "or nots" crept into our personal vocabulary. We learned early on that these choices allowed us to think and live based on our joy, not anyone else's.

We came to realize that in this initial session, she was already working on both of us. The result was that Rev. Deb was going to perform Reiki on me over the next few months or until I was healed from cancer. Once we got home, we immediately took a nap for four hours.

I distinctly remember two questions Rev. Deb asked of me during our first session. The first question was, "What brings you joy?" Without hesitation, I answered that singing brought me joy but I had not done so on a regular basis for about 20 years. She said, "Why not?" I did not have an answer. It became clear to me that I was not doing the one thing in my life that brought me joy… and why not? I started singing with a chorus that September and have not stopped since.

The second question was, "Do you believe you can be healed?" The answer to this did not register right away. I thought of healing regarding someone else or the healings in the Bible, but not me. That got me thinking again. I also did not think of healing as a possibility as my focus had been solely on the scientific and medical evidence and not the spiritual aspect of healing. It took me a good long while to come around to that possibility for myself, but soon I did. Each time we went to the [Reiki] table, she would pray for Jesus and all the saints and ancestors to come into the room. She said many times the room was full. I believed her. They were summoned and working alongside us every time. It was bliss.

In my following sessions, she shaped my word choices, thought processes, spirit, and present being to become abundant and full of joy. A lot of times what she said went over my head or I was too tired to hear, but I knew my spirit heard her and absorbed each blessed nugget.

She performed Reiki on me and allowed the spirits to work on me. I felt something special and divine about these sessions. I remember purple explosions from my closed eyes and many tremors in my torso and legs as energy was released. I came to know that something spiritual in nature was happening to me and had no doubt I was being healed.

We also worked on the root cause of my cancer which to her (and now me) was that it is a disease of anger. My cancer had manifested in the root chakra because of my perceptions around family and love of family. I had much unresolved anger with my family that needed to be dealt with on an internal and spiritual level. Identifying these things was painful and permeated not just this life but past lives as well. I was shocked by this pattern that I needed to break by forgiving all parties involved in these actions, including myself. The healing power of forgiveness was integral in my transformation from deep-seated anger to freeing joy.

There was never a time during this experience that I said this is not right or unnecessary. I was open to it from the start. Open to seeing this spirit world and myself in it differently. The options were endless and free. I was endless and free. I am endless and free.

I am eternally grateful for Rev. Deb as she guided me to a place of healing. The healing of my body, my mind, and my spirit. She will say it was me that healed myself. But without her, I would not have known where to begin with healing myself. We stopped meeting in November of that year when my scans returned a result of "no evidence of cancer" in my body. I am free of cancer and living a life of abundance and joy. This experience was a miracle and so is she.

I explain a miracle as a shift in our lives which cannot be explained by our linear, concrete, 3D mentalities. To me, a miracle is an act of Divine intervention, brought to front and center through co-creation of our belief in our word plus Spirit, no matter how unimportant, frivolous or substantial. What we see is evidence, *an effect of our faith,* knowing of and believing *in what we cannot yet see.* The act of the miracle produces a change in what we see, what we are, how we live, in realizing ourselves as One with the Divine.

Co-creation is an act of choosing to partner with the mystical. We partner with the mystical simply by saying, Yes, I believe You exist. *Yes, I believe there is more in this life. Yes, I know goodness is out there. Yes, I feel health is possible. Yes, I have angels all around me, helping me, nudging me, supporting me. Yes, I can feel my loved ones around me even though they are no longer in physical form. Yes, I believe healing is possible! Yes, I believe the answer will come to me. Yes, I know there is a great job out there for me. Yes, I know the right and wonderful relationship will show up for me. Yes, I know this is temporary and it is possible to find peace here.*

Years ago, a client's husband came to meet with me. His wife had cancer and she felt very positive about our work together. After a healing session for his back pain, he asked me, how do I have faith? I suggested he ask to see something, anything at all, then let it go. He asked to see a cardinal. There were none around their home, so he felt pretty sure it would not work, but he assured me he was willing to remain open. That evening, he and his wife sat on their deck, and two cardinals came and sat on the deck with them. The cardinals stayed for quite a while. His wife called me the next day to tell me the story and how he was speechless. His back was also without pain and he ran the next morning for the first time in many months.

Partnering with the mystical only takes your belief in it. Are you willing? It is all up to you.

17

MANIFESTING HOMES

He said to them, because of your little faith. For truly, I say to you,
if you have faith like a grain of mustard seed, you will say to this
mountain, 'Move from here to there,' and it will move, and nothing
will be impossible for you.
~ Mathew 17:20

◆

know this to be true. **It is done through us according to our**
faith. Our faith, that which we believe about every aspect of life,
is influenced by our perceptions, which are created through our
thoughts. The more we think about anything, the more of it we get.
Metaphysics 101. I have proven this repeatedly, each day of my life.
In fact, I depend on it.

Some would say this is manifesting. I call it understanding
and applying Universal Law. Manifesting sounds like we are creating
it from scratch, whatever it is. Such hard work. I believe everything
is already created, and our understanding of the Laws brings it into
our personal experience, into this three-dimensional touch it, feel
it, see it reality. I believe that what we desire already exists. It is not
creating or manifesting, *so much as drawing that which is already*
created to us. Some call this co-creation. I believe that to co-create
a life of grace and positive fulfillment, it is our work to become fully
and without any doubt (which is a raising of our inner vibration)
aligned with the Universal Law: as above, so below—as within, so
without. This is the Mirror Law; all we see is a reflection of all that
is within us. If we do not like what we see, we can change our
thinking to shift our beliefs, so we will see an outer change.

At one point in my life, I was seeking a new living situation. I
had criteria for an apartment, believing that we ask God for what we

wish to see by aligning our beliefs in its existence before we can see it. I wanted a one-bedroom with hardwood floors, lots of light, freshly painted white, open shelving, new appliances, and off-street parking that also allowed dogs, all for $800 per month in a town where a one-bedroom started at $1,200 and off-street parking was left for million-dollar homes. I know—particular, crazy, picky, or faith-filled?

No such apartments in the newspapers for weeks. When people inquired how I was, how the hunt for this *impossible* apartment was going, I answered that it had not presented itself yet, but I knew it was here. The response was usually, "Oh, good luck with that," stated in that *it will never happen* tone. When I called a realtor I knew to check in and explained what I was looking for, he all but laughed at me. I remained positive. I replied, "I know it exists, I just have to find it." He of course assured me it did not.

Then I found an ad that fit my description. The man I called was very nice, but he had just rented the apartment to someone else. Because he thought I sounded pleasant, he shared with me the number and name of a woman who worked for a well-known local real estate entrepreneur. She was not in her office when I called, so I left her a voice mail with details of what I was looking for. An hour later she called me back, leaving me a phone message that she did have that exact apartment (which she found eerie for I described it to a tee, including fresh white paint not yet dry), but had just accepted a new renter via a phone call. They were going to meet there tomorrow and finalize the deal. If she had anything else come up, she would keep me in mind and call me back.

This made me feel hopeful. I was not disappointed. I felt like I was closer to my desired new home, for now I knew it physically existed! All I wanted *was* possible. I was uplifted.

The next day I received a second call from the same rental agent. I was available, so this time a conversation between us took place.

"It is the strangest thing, Deborah. The woman who wanted it called me back this morning. On her own, she had driven by the address I gave her before we were to meet today. She did not like the way it looked. She decided no. So, do you still want to see it?"

When we met there later the same day, I was dumbfounded. For the past few months, I had walked by this building every day on my way to and from work. A woman always sat on the front porch and we would exchange waves. Yes, the apartment was all I had asked for. When I double-checked about dogs, she said she only takes dogs, no cats. The only time I have ever heard that. She also said no need for a pet deposit, first or last or last month's rent; just pay monthly. *Are you kidding?*

The building was old and in need of some TLC. There was a dilapidated abandoned car in the parking lot area. Yet all I could feel was gratitude. It was perfect.

Within one week of my moving in, the abandoned car in the parking area was towed away. Within one month, the hallway carpets were removed to reveal the beautiful original floors. The outside of the building had started to get a new paint job. No, I had not asked anyone or written any nasty letters or made any requests. Gratitude attracts more to be in gratitude for.

An intriguing moment at this residence took place one morning when I was in the hall outside my first-floor apartment, sweeping the old oak floors. A young man who lived upstairs came down a flight, stopped, and introduced himself. He did not ask what I did. As far as I knew, he knew nothing about me. I had no advertising on my car. He had never been a client. He simply asked why I was sweeping the floor. I answered, "I like to care for my home."

As if we were old friends, he began an immediate conversation regarding a visitation the evening before of what he described as a female ghost, of the friendly persuasion. As he spoke, I could see her, dressed in clothes from the 1930s, including garters and stockings. He asked, did I know anything about this kind of thing? Did I believe in ghosts? His inquiry led to a longer discussion of my kind of house clearing (the cleaning of any unwanted energies or spirits). After I perfectly described his surprise visitor and what she was doing, he was ready to receive valuable advice and tools. I was aware that the house had many souls still residing in it, for it had originally been built in the 1800s as a boarding house for railroad workers. This was the only time this young man and I ever spoke. Oh, and he also asked if I had anything to do with the car being removed, the rugs coming up, and having the building painted. My answer: "I know for sure, being grateful can move mountains."

My husband and I share a mutual love of antique farmhouses. One day I made the conscious choice to try to manifest, or rather, to apply truths to see this dream come into our reality. (At this time in my journey, I was hosting a weekly Abraham-Hicks group.) Yes, this is called the Law of Attraction. How did I go about this? First, I created a vision board. I had photos of old stone walls, pastures, an antique white farmhouse, barns, and a pond. I made a list of the dream elements: sunlight, old worn floors, one hundred fifty to two hundred years old, and an art studio. We lived in northeastern Massachusetts, where these types of homes were common and very expensive.

I had to let go of the cost. We did not have that kind of money. I simply focused on the dream. I went to every open house of any antique home that was listed. My husband refused to go with me because he firmly stated we could not afford it, so it would be no use to look. Bill predominantly sees from his left brain, his "engineering mind." Being more right-brained, I am always seeing a realm of open possibilities not based on linear sight. I enjoyed as many open houses as possible, because these homes make me happy.

Feeling joy is good, yes? I love a home with soul, stories, and history. Walking through homes we could not afford, I never felt jealous or sad. I felt privileged to be seeing them, admiring the rooms, feeling the spirit of an old house. This simply makes me happy.

After about six months of this positive thinking, on New Year's Day, I took the dream board off my wall and put it in the trash. I simply said, "God, I have done all I know to do. I have said every prayer, applied every law of attraction I know, the rest is up to you." I let it go.

Within one week I had a phone call from a dear friend who was a private duty nurse at a two-hundred-year-old private estate. The present caretakers of the property were moving on. My friend thought that I might like to consider being the new caretaker. Was I interested? Another "awe in God" moment. I said yes. She gave us the contact information. Within one month, we had signed a contract to be the new caretakers of our dream home. It was a 24/7 job with a four-bedroom, two-bath living quarters in exchange. We only had to pay for our internet connection.

No, at that time we could never have purchased this fine, historic 1800s farm home. And in truth, in hindsight, I was applying my prayers and manifesting tools to the house, not to the acquiring of money to buy a farmhouse. I had already been to this property once to visit my nursing friend. I knew the location the moment she had given me directions. When I was a child, my mother and I used to drive right by the driveway entrance every Saturday morning on our way to do food shopping. And to top that, the farm was on the road I grew up on, except the street switched names when the town lines changed.

It was quite an amazing private property, set back from the road down an 800-foot driveway. On my original visit, which had been to visit my friend, several owls had greeted me as they all perched in a circle on the single tree in the center of the driveway. Horses were still on the property then, bringing tears to my eyes when I watched them gallop through the snowy pastures. Even though it was an amazing antique farmhouse with a five-story barn and gorgeous pastures and a pond, just like what I was attempting to manifest, *I never thought this property could be the one.*

No, we did not own it, but I treated it and all its inhabitants with love. For a few years, this gorgeous estate was under my care and was our home. I only felt and still feel that it was a privilege.

At the end of our time at the farm, we were given four months to find our new home. Spirit made it clear that we were to buy a house. The first house we saw, we loved. It seemed perfect for me to have a home office and was near the main routes for my husband's commute. We were led to believe the owner had already bought her new home, so we made an offer that day. It was accepted. Wow, so easy!

The next day my son, our dealmaker, came to tell us he had news. He had been on the phone with the owner and her lawyer. Her deal had fallen through, so our deal fell through. Not so easy after all.

The second house I fell in love with had a barn for my art studio. Melt my heart. The house was small, but I could make it work. We offered full price. The ninety-seven-year-old owners' son was handling the sale. Because he was mad at their realtor for lowering the price the month before, and even though we offered full price, he came back to us asking for ten thousand dollars more. The realtor apologized profusely. "No thank you," I stated. Not meant to be ours.

The next house my son and I drove to together in a snowstorm to view. He had been finding the houses for us, but I had found this one myself. I loved it. It had not been lived in for over a year. The 1930s radiators had all been taken off the walls, the water turned off, and it was a cold, lonely vintage house with original features throughout. The moment I walked in, I was in love. I said nothing. We went back to the car and my son turned to me. "Mom, why do you love broken things?"

My husband and I went back two days later. The realtor sent his young assistant, who was brand new at this type of work. My husband had to shovel a path through the snow because the assistant was in heels. We entered the house and I let my husband stroll. He opened a kitchen cabinet, discovering a dead mouse. The realtor-in-training screamed. I assured her this was a nonissue for us. I had been a caretaker in a two-hundred-year-old house with critters, so this was not a problem. She apologized some more. My husband said okay, let's make an offer.

Our offer was refused. I felt strongly this was our home. The red house on the hill. It was refused with no negotiation. (To be honest, the offer included some creative financing.) Okay, onward. Give it to God. No other home came close to the feeling I experienced when I first walked in. I moved on. Let it go, Deborah. Trust.

It was time to find our new home, as our time at the farm was coming to an end.

One house we saw had an incredibly low purchase price with ugly do-it-yourself projects throughout ample square footage (although I knew I could alter them). We went back to the house three times. I made a deliberate effort, but it was not our home. My husband agreed.

Another house my son loved was brand new. It needed nothing. Not for me.

The next house was an amazing mid-century modern. (I appreciate any home architecturally relevant.) We made the offer. Accepted. Then, I had emergency gall bladder surgery. Six days later we had the house inspection. Out of 144 points, it passed only four. We came back to the owner with *only* a request for a structural engineer. Denied. The deal fell through. Okay now. Let's regroup.

I remember laughing when people asked if I was discouraged. No, only God could be doing this, providing all these odd and rather ridiculous reasons for deals falling through. I knew there was most definitely a bigger plan at work here. I just had no idea what it was.

The night before we were going to have to reapply for our mortgage, I asked my husband if he would revisit the red house (with the mouse) with me. He said, make the deal. In an hour we had a contract.

The house inspection showed a couple of items we made requests on, not inexpensive, and the owner agreed. All was going smoothly.

Because of our time parameters, the owner had kindly permitted me to clean the house before we closed. On the first day of cleaning two friends helped me. It was wonderful to see the yard without snow. The second day of cleaning was the morning of our scheduled two o'clock closing. A long-term student of mine and I arrived at 8:00 a.m. As we drove into the driveway, she started laughing. The entire front yard was dug up, from the house to the road. A large tractor sat amidst substantial mounds of dirt. Two men with neon-green water department shirts were staring into a vast hole, evidently contemplating what was next.

I parked. I walked over to these two gentlemen. "Good morning."

The town's water superintendent looked at me. "Are you the new owner?"

Pretending I had a watch on my wrist, I glanced down. "Not yet."

"I can't tell you anything."

"Okay then, let me ask this. Whatever *this* is (using wide elaborate hand gestures for effect), who is financially responsible, the town or the homeowner?"

It took a few moments, some shoulder shrugging and glances between them before the superintendent looked at me and answered, "The homeowner."

"Thank you both."

And I walked back to the car and called their realtor.

The owner would pay for everything. Due to the cost of these unforeseen water pipe repairs and lawn care, combined with the already paid-for new oil tank and foundation work, as we had negotiated, they needed one month or more before they could close on the sale of the house. It would not be happening today, as scheduled. They kindly (and legally with a codicil added to the agreement), let us choose the closing date. I kept my moving schedule. We moved in one month before it was legally ours. They did not charge us rent. The town had water working by the day we moved in.

I felt it was our home from the moment I first saw it. Oh, and if they had accepted our first offer during a snowy winter, this leak would never have been discovered. We would not have been able to afford to fix it ourselves. So, God *did* know best. Refuse the first offer. As well as, no other home will be successfully purchased, for any number of reasons. Because this *is* the one. Sometimes God is the great arranger, the ultimate fixer. "*Okay, I hear you, let me see what I can do.*"

Manifesting in your own life, meaning applying your faith to bring to you what you cannot yet see in form, is not only possible, *but what you are already doing.* We are each manifesting each moment. We are made of creative God-stuff. Co-creating and manifesting is part of our Divine programming. Some begin their day by running late and complaining, then the entire day will bring more for them to complain about. Some live in the past by telling stories over and over and wonder why the present is not a pleasant experience. Others awake and verbally claim their good for a day of extraordinary joy, and have that. Remember, we attract through *both* fear and love. The universe responds to your vibration. Your cells respond to your stories. You are a creating genius, own it. Be empowered by it. In this life and the next!

18

PAST LIVES

We are travelers on a cosmic journey, stardust, swirling and dancing in the eddies and whirlpools of infinity. Life is eternal. We have stopped for a moment to encounter each other, to meet, to love, to share. This is a precious moment. It is a little parenthesis in eternity.

~ Paul Coelho, THE ALCHEMIST

◆

Let me begin by saying I am not as positive in defining past lives as I am in other experiences. Are there past lives, as in reincarnation over and over again, or are we living quantum lives, multiple lives across fields of realities all happening at the same time? If so, what about parallel lives? I accept all of these. I believe that our soul, our true identity, does live repeatedly in different human bodies as we choose to reincarnate on earth. I have had too many regression experiences to not believe. I do believe in karma, from life to life as well as moment to moment; we receive what we give, we sow what we seed.

I also believe in quantum lives, or perhaps experiences. Too often I have felt myself living another existence, feeling called to show up differently than what I am in this life. More than a feeling, it is an ache, as if a part of myself is disconnected, or lost. This experience is in the past for me today. I fully embrace who and what I am now. I have not felt the call to express differently for several years. Perhaps, for those who do feel this angst now, you can believe that it is all part of the onion peeling away, revealing ourselves as One being, fully embodied in this life and all others.

I have known, in the depths of my heart, somewhere I am an artist. I am convinced quantum particles of who I am are an artist, somewhere. Since a young age, I have enjoyed multiple artistic expressions in my life, from the theater, acting, and playwriting to painting, drawing, and other mediums. The call to it, the comfort to it, the natural knowing of it is palpable—yet it has not been how I could see myself making a living or expressing fully. My painting, although it has sold through the years, comes and goes. It is more than a hobby for me, it is a way of expressing myself, as is my chosen purpose as a spiritual teacher, counselor, and healer. Art is a language I understand. Creating, I understand. My husband Bill says my entire life is my palette—our home, our yard, a canvas, whatever I do, he sees me doing from an artistic heart.

I feel very different when I am painting than when I am doing my healing work. It may feel like I am in a different body, a different mindset, but of the same heart. To my awareness, I have never had a past life as an artist. The same experience is true for me in expressing in church ministry, as was my plan, my yearning, and dream for ten years. My unmanifested desire to be hired to lead a physical church congregation was a most painful and palpable journey. After church denials to be more than a guest speaker or interim minister, I was brought to my knees. To my knowledge, each congregation loved me and I, them. Our bonds were and remain incredibly gratifying. Comments were made, such as "We sell more CDs of your services than any others." and "More people attend your workshops than any we ever hosted."

There were two final blows, each one getting more and more painful as I felt this *is* what I am to do. Of course, the pain increased as I defiantly, stubbornly, and willfully kept trying. One rejection came after three years of sporadically serving a community, being supported fully by their outgoing minister, and consistently leading them for most of the final year. Despite all this, the board denied my inquiry to become their full-time minister. Their response to me as I remember was: *"Although they had learned much from me, and the congregation had grown and we were having a love fest; I was not ordained through their particular teaching resulting in people could not get credits for the classes."* This was an astonishingly painful wallop to my heart. I was shocked. I felt like a balloon that had the air sucked out of it. This was unimaginable to me, given the obvious mutual love and the success we had all experienced together. I was stunned.

At the time, I could not make sense of their choice. My husband and I were in the middle of moving and had not yet firmed up new housing, for we were both sure I would be offered the position. I remember walking out of the church after the meeting, down the stairs to the parking lot. I am sure I left my body. I prayed to my angels to drive me home.

The blessing for me in this particular experience was that I found strength through integrity. Several congregants stayed in touch with me. On one particular day, I received a call from Rosie, sharing that there had been a church meeting the previous evening, with people being vocal about me not being hired. Her brave six-year-old had stood and spoken up for Rev. Deb. How precious to me. Yet, I can remember taking a big breath and responding to her, "Rosie, your board made a decision they believe in. They want the very best for you all. It is true, you would not receive credit for classes from me, and they evidently could not see a way around that. They are doing the best they are able. No, I cannot call them, this is your church, you all need to work together to do what is best for the entire community." I felt I empowered her as I redirected her back to her community, even while my heart was broken.

The final blow to this dream and my ego was when I and a recently ordained student I had mentored into divinity school were up for the same post. On the linear plane, I had church experience, he had none. My mentor had told me point-blank I could not be a minister at her associated church for I was not ordained by the same community. Neither was he. I had offered nine outstanding letters of recommendation, had served this church off and on for a few years, all in excellent standing and what I felt was a deep respect and mutual admiration. As I sat alone in my office one day, the call came in; they had offered the young man who was void of ministerial leadership experience the position. He had accepted.

I can feel my body sink in reliving this moment. The emotions I felt were palpable, excruciating, confusing, and befuddled. I think I was in shock. I do not remember even crying. I called a friend, who was too busy to go out with me and process. Devasted at that moment, clarity struck. This was between me and God.

I spent the afternoon by myself, pondering, praying, and seeking understanding. I was numb. I had expected different. There was nowhere else I felt more myself, at home, than when I was preaching, orating, talking, in celebration with others. I loved it. I had found my spot. I was comfortable in front of hundreds of people; that was never an issue for me. I knew if I was at a super church of thousands, I would feel the same. Any service I had ever done, Sunday or wedding or funeral, people were consistently generous with their expressions of gratitude. At this time in my life, leading a church was my dream. I felt it was my calling.

Later that day, Spirit directed me to a particular book. I do not remember the title. I thought, "Okay God, what?" I let the book fall open to a random page, which in my memory, read, "Many times, what you so desperately want in your human life and cannot achieve is what you do when home on the other side. You will not reach that while in human form." It went on about the palpable memory, the depth of the calling… and the not reaching it in the present life on earth.

Yes! This must be it. This resonated with me. In my sleep later that evening, I was shown my life on the other side. I was accessing a motion picture of me, in male form, speaking with thousands, but on the other side, in Heaven, or Home, as I call it.

My ultimate joy. I experienced relief in the acknowledgment of this deep calling that went beyond any other I have had. To see and feel that I am doing this, that this is me, was pure liberation. How this works through physics I have no idea, but I saw myself at Home, speaking, in the present tense. No wonder I wanted to fulfill this dream to lead a church so very much, felt the pull to this calling, to speak to many each Sunday. No wonder.

The conclusion to this story is, before the hiring decision had been made, I had been previously scheduled to speak at the church that had not hired me. Yes, that is correct. As Bill said, "Honey, anyone will understand if you back out." No, that was not my way. Now, for the raise-it-up-higher spiritual calling kick in the pants: the date I was on the calendar to speak was the first Sunday of the new minister's tenure. Yup, he had the day off.

I did it. I went. It was much more than awkward. Hidden faces. People ignoring me. I felt privileged to speak any Sunday in a church, grateful to have the opportunity. On this particular Sunday, I wanted to prove to myself that I could show up in love in uncomfortable circumstances, that my ego was not running the show, trusting fully that God sees the whole picture and that I do not, not yet. Before I went to the podium to begin the actual Sunday message, I stood on the ground level with the chairs, directly with the congregation. "Yes, today feels awkward for many of us, but we can do this…" and whatever else I said, just as the newly hired minister came running down the aisle. Yes, he ran. He was late. This gave me a too-good-to-pass-up joke opportunity about him not only having his first day on the new job off but being late on his first day. It broke the tension, and we got on with our Sunday.

I found the most difficult and awkward fellowship following this service to be an embarrassing experience. I was standing at the edge of the room, gazing upon these people I had wanted to join with, to build community with, and now I was not even being politely acknowledged. (It was a bad movie, that now I realize I

148

created, but then, I was staring, perhaps with my mouth open, because I could not look away at what felt like insanity to me.) What was happening? Board members did not speak with me, come over to me, look me in the eye, or even say goodbye. No handshakes, no hugs, no recognition, no kindness extended at all. Everyone rallied around the new minister. Of course, he was their new minister, and it was his first day.

I left, to my eyes unnoticed, and went to my car. I sat, preparing to drive away from this congregation I had served off and on for over two years, for the final time. "Dear God, thank you for getting me through this morning," I told God I give up. I get it. I stop here, now, no more attempts, dreams, or longings to have a ministerial church position. I got it. I will never try again. This is enough. God, you are too big for one church. Help me to remember, I am doing this, but at Home. With this as my inner guidance, I was able to let go, un-cling, and move forward in a sense of freedom. Thank you for the clarity.

How do I feel I created this experience? We must be brave enough and have enough faith in the laws of the universe to do the emotional excavation within ourselves that it may take to see why. What is or was the belief I am holding, the belief I value, that has brought this experience to me? I looked at that. And what I found when I dug deep enough was that I did feel their choice, Alan, was the best choice for them. Why? He lived near the church. He lived in Boston, I lived nearly an hour away, a longer drive during traffic any other day of the week but Sunday. As I looked at this, I remembered thinking, how can I fully serve this community I do not live in? Or at least, closer to? How could I serve shut-ins, make hospital visits, or attend meetings with ease? Maybe Alan is the best choice for the community. I had considered this, and I realized I put more value on his easy access than I put on my abilities. In hindsight, I am pleased I valued the community and what was best for them rather than me being the right one.

The first past life regression I experienced was spontaneous. I was reading *Out on a Limb* (1983), a transformational book written by actress Shirley MacLaine. I could not read it fast enough. I felt a profound connection with her and the remarkable experiences she shared. I still remember getting up from my couch and going into my bedroom to nap. I sat on the edge of my bed, which had me looking directly into my vanity mirror, and there I/she was. A young girl, ten years old, dressed up to look like a boy, in a Confederate soldier's uniform, just floating in my mirror staring at me. She was physically, humanly present. She was me. How did I know? All I can say is: You just know.

She did not stay long. We conversed telepathically, she showed me that in this past life I had experienced being a gutsy little girl whose parents had died. I "knew" that to be safe, I/she had to pretend to be a boy during this wartime, without any adults to protect her. Meeting her gave me inner strength. She instantly reminded me of what I am made of. At that time in my present life, I was newly divorced, in my first apartment, attempting to ride out this challenge of making ends meet, sharing joint custody of my child, and being single again after ten years. Seeing her and meeting her gave me encouragement no one else could have. Eternally dear to me, thank you.

(In proofreading this book, one day I looked up *young girls, civil war, dressed up as boys*. It was a thing! It was a choice and was done for safety reasons. My mind had no linear awareness of this historical fact, but my soul did.)

As a child, I suffered from a skin ailment, eczema. Dry, itchy, and to the degree I had it, painful. Appearing instantly allergic to many different household soaps, cleaners, and even lobster juice, it was a very unpleasant experience. Skin creams and soaking in chemicals was the standard procedure in the late 1950s and early 1960s. Throughout first grade, I wore little white gloves with the tips cut off to hold the heavy-duty steroid applications on my cracked and bleeding skin. Every afternoon after school I had to soak my hands in a solution that allowed me some relief and movement. It took many years for my eczema to fully go away, leaving first grade and being newly married as the times of my worst outbreaks. As a newlywed at age nineteen, I had a severe occurrence of eczema all over my body. I was in daily pain. My facial skin looked like the Sahara Desert, flaking, peeling, and crumbling to the point that my boss, as I worked in retail, sent me home one day and directed me to go to a doctor. This was not a good look for selling dresses.

I decided to go see a new doctor of my choosing, not the family one from childhood. This new dermatologist told me I could never cure it and that while it would never go away, I could learn to control it. I remember thinking, *watch me, yes, I can.*

At this time, I delved into nutrition. I knew the skin to be the largest organ, so in my mind, this had to be an inside job. I did learn about drinking more water (this was before it was a well-known daily requirement) and eating so I would not dehydrate my skin. I learned to hydrate myself through healthy food choices. I learned that caffeine, chocolate, and carbonated soft drinks all dehydrated skin. Yes, with these changes the eczema began to retreat. For several years I had only small unseen patches over my body, and soaps and some clothing would still irritate me. But it went fully away and has stayed away since my first professional past life regression session.

My first scheduled, professional past life regression experience brought me back to a lifetime as a young man named David. The practitioner was a friend; consequently, I was fully comfortable, relaxed, and without any resistance, which allowed for a profound and clear regression. Now, David had always been a name I felt drawn to. It was always the name I thought I would want if I had been a boy. The time frame of this life was BC, very early, in the area of what was Mesopotamia. (I have no human knowledge of ancient civilizations or maps.) In this lifetime, I was a dark-haired, emaciated young man in my mid-twenties. Beggar-like. I had stolen jewelry from my mother and, feeling guilty, I was on my way back to return the jewels. I knew that I had to break into my parent's seaside home to do so. I then watched myself running from my wealthy family's guards. Plunging into the water I went, landing on a raft I had premade from broken timbers, tying them together with rope as my getaway vehicle. Drifting out to sea, I died from literally being burned by the sun. I was dehydrated, crisp, and looked like a piece of meat. It was gruesome.

Through this courage to look at what had been, I was given information that answered many questions. My skin, for one, and eczema specifically. In my present life, as a young swimmer, I was outside all summer long. I burned instantly. Eventually, I would get surprisingly dark, but initially, I would burn to a crisp and freckle as if I was speckled with paint. I still have hyperpigmentation, dry skin, and respectfully protect myself from the sun. Once, a few years ago, I was hospitalized due to dehydration on a busy day of errands. The second bit of information that shined a welcome light on my present life was the fact that my family had disowned me in this David life because I did not want their wealthy material lifestyle. This was the same theme for me in this lifetime. I shunned my parent's materialism and was disowned, even if for a short time; the language still applied.

Nothing is ever physically painful during a past life regression. You can see, watch or experience your death, accidents, and more without the pain. However, we do feel the feelings of our experience on an empathetic level. The experience is felt, minus the fear and emotional attachment. Understanding comes alive. Through this, forgiveness takes place. This experience causes an unlodging of the present story in our energy field. It will no longer need repeating in a future incarnation.

I learned through past life regressions that being a human is not the only choice we have. No, I do not believe we can come back as animals. I was stunned the day my session brought me back to a life as a spark of light. I awoke in thick, dark, gooey mud. I darted here and there, breaking up the mud, opening the darkness to the light. This was my purpose. This was for a very short period, not as many years as human life. How do I know it was me? The best explanation is when watching a past life, we instantly know the character as ourselves, through a connection, a sameness.

My most profound past life experience in conjunction with my present life was with Jenn. We first met at her college graduation. I was present in the dining room, for I was on the alumni board of my alma mater, while the graduate luncheon was taking place. It was hard to understand why not every single eye was on her. A tall blonde beauty with an elfin face, she walked with ease and confidence on high heels that made her equal to the 6' 4" college president as they chatted. Who is she, I wondered. When it was appropriate, I went to her and introduced myself.

We became instant friends. I was invited to her family's home the next day for her post-graduation celebration. Nothing had felt more natural to me. Jenn was an artist. Certainly, similar souls. We naturally laughed together, connected, and the entire time, I wondered, *Why? How have I only known you for just over twenty-four hours?*

Fourteen years later was the next time I saw Jenn when she walked into my newly formed gallery in 1992 to show me her artwork. Time stopped and laughter prevailed.

I chose to carry her photography and accepted an invitation to view her paintings at her home studio. She was doing a series on personal icons. Jenn lived in the same neighborhood as my maternal grandmother had, where my mother had grown up. It was familiar. Jenn gave me a tour, then we entered her studio, I stood back from the easel, as requested, because she wanted to talk about the work first, then dramatically remove the sheet so I could see the icon of her choice. In talking about the work, she was not specific about who it was, but simply that her heart had opened as she painted. The sheet came away and Jesus was starring right at me. I have no memory of what went thru my mind, but I had to leave the room. I apologized, left her studio, left the house, and drove away. I could not be present there. In as few words as possible, I freaked out.

The path to our ongoing-ness is unclear for me. I remember that Jenn and I met with our children for pizza, her daughter, and my son. I know my gallery continued to carry her photography. I know one night I was on a date and walked into a bar and Jenn was sitting at a window table with her date, the same man I had been out with the weekend before. I know that a local businessman had come into my gallery one day while Jenn and I were visiting, and he invited us to join him in a ménage à trois. We said no. Ours was a unique chemistry.

At my next past life regression appointment, I learned I had been a man, a soldier named David, at the time of the Holy Wars, and Martin Luther. (Yes, another lifetime as a David.) Remember, I know nothing about historical facts, this information comes to us during a regression through an innate knowing and inner awareness. To this day, I recall the experience. In the late 1500s, I was on a horse, leading my men. We stopped in front of a castle that sat on a hill. I knew I was Catholic. There was a young woman, Elisabeth.

(At this point, it was of unknown importance for me to recognize the S, instead of a Z in her name.) She was blonde and ran down the hill to me. We were deeply in love, but she was Protestant. This was not a welcomed relationship at this time in history. Our love was forbidden. As we hugged, an arrow was shot into Elisabeth. She died in my arms. I watched myself, collapsed on the hillside, holding her body against my armor, as blood poured over me from her wound. I could and still do feel the devastation of that moment.

Coming back into the present time and space after the regression, I felt the depths of love these two beings shared. I knew it was Jenn. Elisabeth was now Jenn in this lifetime. Same soul. I knew it. I was certain.

I immediately drove back to the gallery and called her. (this was in pre-cell phone days.) I told Jenn the story of my past life session. Through her tears, she told me she was coming to the gallery to tell me more.

Her daughter's first word was Elisabeth (with an S, not a Z). It had always seemed so very odd to Jenn. Not "Momma" or anything simple. Elisabeth. They knew no one named Elisabeth or Elizabeth. Then, Jenn gave me a few pages of paper to read. Her daughter had recently written a story for her English class. It was the story of a young blonde girl called Elisabeth in love with an ancient warrior named David. The princess had been killed by an arrow. She had died in the arms of the man she loved. It was our story.

I realize this is unbelievable. You have my word this is my truth. We sat there in awe, thankful to be given this information. And perhaps now, the idea that Jenn had painted Jesus and I could not be in the same room with her made some sense. At that point, I had yet to develop my intimate faithful relationship with Jesus, as I do now. (In January 2021, while editing, I curiously checked up on Martin Luther on Wikipedia. I never had before. I found that he and his wife's first child was named Elisabeth and did not survive infancy.)

When the gallery/healing center closed, Jenn and I said goodbye. Our next meeting was one I believe she was unaware of. Jenn was with a man I knew, a well-known business owner in our town, whose first wife would be a client and his daughter my student many years later. The cosmic web continually unfolding. Jenn and that man sat in front of me at a theater production. When they walked out, I stood up from my aisle seat to meet her, but she looked right through me, as if she did not see, know or recognize me. Not a glance or a blink. I was nonexistent. All I remember thinking was she was in love and happy. This is good.

Many years later, as a healer, I was at a local hospice with a client and her family. The family had asked me to not go into my client's room since the nurses were trying to calm her. This was unusual for me. Families want me with their loved ones, believing I would be the one to calm them down, but this family knew not of my work. I respected their wishes. Sitting at a table in the front hall of the hospice, awaiting permission to be with my client to help her to transition to her next life, I asked God, why? I had never been asked by a family to *not* sit with their beloved. If they will not let me be with her, why am I here? And just as I asked, the man whom I had seen Jenn with at the theater years before walked through the front door of the hospice, with urgency on his face. I knew. I watched him walk to a room. It was Jenn. I walked past the room to read the patient's name, to verify my knowing. Here I was, with her again, as she transitioned. I sat in prayer, I stood near her room. I sent my love from afar.

I found her obituary two days later. Yes, she had died the day I was at the hospice. She died the day I was outside her door. Once again, I was in awe of this thing we call life and the eternalness of it all. Divine perfection. Thank you, Jenn. Thank you, God, for the constant reassurance of Your existence. I look forward to it every day.

In my private practice as a healer, one of the most interesting findings regarding past lives has been that of what one may call star-crossed lovers. I have encountered a few cases where siblings had an incestuous relationship and through past life regressions learned they had been lovers and/or spouses in previous lives. In one case in particular it had been ongoing since they were teenagers until they fell in love with other people and both married. It was never an issue, never anything they felt guilty about. Their incestuous relationship never harmed anyone else. It simply was. Into adulthood they became and were best of friends, sharing family holidays with no hint of any other relationship or history. When my client witnessed herself and her sibling in a previous life as husband and wife, this gave her even more clarity regarding this hidden secret which had never been discussed with anyone, until then.

Seeing our past lives allows us to truly know we have all walked in one another's shoes. I know people who have discovered they were a murderer, a scam artist, the abuser of their presently abusive boyfriend. This helps us to grow in compassion and have less judgment. Also, when we see who we have been, and how our loved ones play repeated roles in our many lives, we can rest assured we will see one another again, after we transition from this life. We also learn that when we can consciously change the story in this lifetime, we do not have to repeat the relationship. How does this work?

There was a time in my life people would call me Barbara, no matter how often I corrected them. At one particular job, several employees did this. These people and I had nothing in common, no pleasant energetic connection at all, yet they simply said to me, *you seem like Barbara to me.* Each connection felt very cold.

One day I asked a friend who was a medium about this. I learned I had lived a shameful life as a woman who physically harmed other people. The people who could not get my name straight had been my victims. This is a horrible story to bring to light; even sharing this publicly is painful. But, as with all stories we carry, there is a way to heal it, to complete it, to stop the cycle. One day a woman unknown to me reached out and instead of using Deborah, she addressed the letter to Barbara. The inside said, "Dear Barbara." I forget why or what the letter was about, but I wrote her back stating my truth; that she knew my name as Deborah and that I have learned through past life work that anyone who refers to me as Barbara, well, it is not a good match.

No one has called me Barbara since.

19

ANIMAL TOTEMS AND MESSENGERS

All things share the same breath—the beast, the tree, the man.
The air shares its spirit with all the life it supports.

~ Chief Seattle

◆

ruth: the animal kingdom has generously shared with me. Each day, my heart pulses with gratitude for their clarity, generosity, and willingness. I look to the animal kingdom for messages from the nonphysical mystery which ties us all together, connecting us in this web of existence.

The vulture is one of my animal totems, one of my power animals. Totems are animals we have a strong bond with, and for the shaman, share similar attributes with. After my mother passed, I spent a month in Florida closing, packing, shipping, clearing, cleaning, and preparing my parents' home for sale. My sister had come to help. The day we left, we locked up the house, said goodbye, and headed for the airport. My sister drove. We were pretty much in silence until we spotted a few vultures by the right-hand side of the road, pecking at a dead animal. I had never seen a vulture before. I was in awe, wondering why they were showing themselves to me at such a poignant time, even as my sister gasped in fear, verbally stating her vile disgust for them. I knew the vultures were a Divine message for me, a gift from Spirit. All I could do was face them and smile.

Upon arriving home, I read the vulture's message as a powerful animal totem, representing birth and death, the natural order of things, as well as new beginnings. (How perfect.) They represent energy, prophecy, Love of the Mother Goddess, and protection. Known as caretakers of the Universe, they rarely kill, unless an animal is already suffering. They pick up after the prey has died. They care for the earth. Caretakers, yes. Thank you, Spirit. Thank you, Mom. Message received. It felt like, *job well done, my good and faithful child.*

I once was the caretaker on a two-hundred-year-old forty-acre non-working farm. The elderly owner, a woman who had never married and whose family had owned the estate for nearly one hundred years, had round-the-clock nursing assistance when I was hired to live on the property and oversee everything nonmedical. This was a magical time for the entire staff. We each loved the farm, its spirit, and the opportunity to be part of it. When the beloved owner made her transition, I stayed on for two more years, assisting the historical society that inherited the property to prepare it for sale, as well as to help the trust that oversaw the estate to clean out the house. This included getting belongings, all furniture, thousands of books, artwork, and every inch of this fine New England estate turned over to new owners through the will directives and bequests, plus working with universities and museums. To give you a clear idea of the immensity of this job, the farm included a five-story barn, a very large outbuilding with a theater, a 5,200 square-foot home, and the land with multiple outbuildings, sheds, and paddocks that required care for the sale. After the work of cleaning, sorting, and overseeing objects was complete, and after two years of filling a large residential dumpster every two weeks, I then called one of the junk hauling companies. Five strong men, one week, and eighteen loads in a fifteen-cubic-yard construction dumpster later, this massive job was complete. The afternoon I took the very last bags of trash from the house to put in the dumpster, I walked out the back door and three vultures, caretakers of the earth, circled above my head. Not threatening. Like a graceful wave, they went in a majestic circle directly over me. I received their presence as a blessing from Spirit: *job well done*. A few circles and they flew away. Thank you, message received. I have never seen vultures at any other time but during my two soul contracts of caretaking: at my parents' home and at the farm.

I also have the deer totem. Deer are highly sensitive with strong intuition, the power to deal gracefully through challenges, and trusting of one's instincts. Deer are always with me. The first week we lived at the farm, my husband was playing his guitar and singing in the living room. Three deer came to the windows. Two stood looking directly into the room, while one lay on the grass, listening to his serenade. When he stopped singing, they gently left. They were welcoming us to our new abode.

Moving to our present home from the farm, Bill and I spoke of how we would miss the deer. We would no longer be in the middle of forty acres. I remember asking my husband if deer language could carry through the waves so new deer may know to welcome us here. During our first week in our new home, one deer was in our driveway, hanging out, munching, stopping to stare at me as I stood at a window, casually enjoying this sacred hello. The same week, in the early morning, when I opened our front door, I heard the sound of multiple hooves before I saw several deer galloping by our stream. Stunning! When I thanked them for greeting us, that evening we watched them feeding in a field directly across from our home. We have not seen them in the field, our driveway, or by the stream for over six years. Often, we see them passing through our wooded backyard where they may stop and simply stare at me from afar. Thank you. Your blessings continually fill my heart.

I also carry the medicine of the hawk, seeing things from a higher perspective. When we were on vacation at the Grand Canyon, my human fear of heights kicked in, so I sat and called on hawk magic. Feeling wings upon my arms, when I remembered to do so, all fear left me. I could stand steady and gaze. Once while standing in the backyard of my husband's childhood home, a hawk flew towards us, coming to us from behind me and sweeping by my cheek with its wing as it took flight right by my head. I heard the whoosh! There is no doubt the hawk has blessed me with the ability of higher sight. On our land, we have a hawk who nests in a tall pine, and very often when I am outside, it will circle above me, as even my husband has noticed.

Not all animals are our power animals; some are simply messengers. Messengers may come to us in dreams or altered realities to bring us information, answer a prayer or offer guidance. I have been blessed with messages in dream time or meditation from White Buffalo, Polar Bear, Black Panther, and Black Bear at certain times of my journey. Each message profound, exactly what I needed at that moment. A miracle. Divine intervention.

Many years ago, I chose to no longer use an alarm clock. I did not want the electricity so close to me; I wanted to trust that I could ask Spirit to awaken me when needed. The first night I did this, I had a workshop to travel to the next day, so I asked Spirit that I be awoken at 4:00 a.m. I trusted and went to sleep.

The next morning, in a fearful startle, I sprang from sleep due to a disturbing nightmare about a mole, not a particularly attractive critter, pushing its head out from the dirt with his nose directly into my face! After five seconds of immediate fluster shock, I glanced at my husband's alarm clock on his side of the bed; it was *exactly* 4:00 a.m. My bother instantly turned to loving gratitude. I laughed out loud. Of course, Spirit moved through this sweet, ugly, bothersome visitor to frighten me awake from a sound rest. What is so perfect is the mole is naturally close to blind and feels his way through the earth. A blind animal waking me up from slumber because I asked to no longer have to see the time but to simply know. And yes, I have never used an alarm clock since, nor a clock by my bed. I trust. And I am never late.

My son was facing a difficult challenge. Because he was now an adult, I hesitated to jump in with my motherly input, or loving interference. In my morning prayers, I asked God for guidance. What was mine to do? When dressed, I went outdoors on a beautiful spring morning to admire the dawn. I love first early morning light, the radiance of the sun before it boldly shows itself fully. An unusual, never-heard-before rustling by the stream in our woods caught my ear. I could see something moving along, close to the ground. It was white in color and foreign to me. I watched this unknown animal move towards the back of our garage, losing my view of it. Wondering where it went and what it was, I opened the door and stepped into our yard, having sight of the garage. There it came, an opossum. Not cute, not small, but the size of a large groundhog. It faced me directly, obviously coming to me, with its classic beady eyes, walking with undeniable intent along the backside of our garage. I had never seen an opossum before. I knew nothing about them.

As it continued to walk determinedly to me, I chose a potential exit route and stood by the backdoor porch entrance. Just in case. It came within two feet of me and stopped. (Whew.) The entire time it was looking directly at me. I thanked it and I went indoors. It left just as it had come. Its work was complete. I have never seen it or other opossums since. Opossum tells you to lie low, do nothing, take a passive stance in your life and all relationships. It also tells you to allow the fire to pass. Okay, message received. I did just that. No motherly interfering.

The morning my mother crossed through the veils, her fudge-colored poodle Brownie and I sat with her. He knew to lay still on the bed, but keep a distance from her, simply shining love and support on this human he adored. He had already said goodbye to my father seven months earlier, and now my mother. When she had taken her final breath, Brownie had in perfect timing raised himself and looked at me. I spoke.

"She's gone, Brownie. She's gone home now."

This incredible dog looked directly at me, then looked up to and through the ceiling, then looked at Mom's body. He did this deliberately distinct act three times, jumped off the bed to the floor, and pranced out of the room.

As I was coming into what I thought was the home stretch of this manuscript, I was struggling with focus, wrestling to clearly explain indescribable mystical experiences. Through language, how can I possibly give worth to partnering with the mystical? I was feeling determined, yet defeated at the moment. In the quest for like communion, I posted this question to on an online writers' group I am part of: "Who knew that one could spend hours trying to decipher what one is attempting to state clearly in one single paragraph?" This group is filled with experienced, make-a-living-at-writing writers. Each one is much more seasoned than I. The replies were wonderful and deeply appreciated by this novice amazed by the hours we can spend, and the doubt we can have. After sitting with each of the comments I experienced a palpable feeling of brand-new energy within me, of feeling renewed to go back to the keyboard again. I stood up from my chair and walked into our kitchen for coffee. It was midmorning. Glancing towards the window, I noticed right that there on our kitchen rug, was a snake. He/she was resting in the warmth. It was not small, either; no doubt when stretched out it was two-plus feet. We have no pets; nothing had brought it inside. It looked quite comfortable. No, we never before had a snake in the house. This was a unique experience.

I yelled for Bill and after a "whoa," he gathered a cardboard box and stick, picked up the snake, causing it obvious disturbance from its nap because *then* it began to wiggle... and took it out to the woods. Yes, for the rest of the day I cautiously looked into the kitchen before entering, even though there was no logical, linear explanation of how this would have come to be. Of course, I immediately looked up the snake as Spirit messenger.

I was already aware that snake is associated with health, Kundalini (the life force that lies coiled at the base of the spine), being grounded, and the shedding of the old. On this day what came to me via the internet universe was that Snake says to you "the *mystical* will become the norm and is called upon when *the singular focus is needed to achieve your goals*." What a perfect message. Exactly what I was hoping to accomplish. Exactly what I needed to hear to complete this manuscript. Thank you, Snake—even though it was uncomfortable to have you show up in our home.

20

CONCLUSION

◆

As many spiritual teachers have taught us, we only have right now, this moment. The now when you read this will be different than my now moment in this present instance. Learn to make the very most of your nows, my friend, for they pave the way for every other moment yet to come.

I am in deep recognition of my life, that if I had not been courageous enough to put my faith in a Higher Power, I never would have made the choices I did, nor would I have had the multitude of different environments in which to have each of these incredible experiences. I would be living an entirely different life. If I had not known to listen deeply, and then trust enough to follow the guidance, this book would not exist. Deep faith rarely happens overnight—for we are a process. In my process, I made a conscious decision to put my faith in God, and the incredible-ness life has to offer us, first. It was and is a slow and steady commitment. Every single choice we make matters. Every single crossroads brings us to the next one. Each moment we choose love over fear, and faith over vacancy, we change.

My life has been called restless by some. For many years a common question from others was, "So, Deborah, what are you doing *now?*"—with emphasis on the ***now*** (in that ridiculing tone).

I learned later in life that my mother used to tell her friends *she wished I would settle down.* To me, once I opened to my calling, with geriatric care and hospice as a jumping-off point to Reiki training and my first healing center, I always thought I was doing the same thing, as I am right now, thirty-five years later, just in a different scenario: caring and caregiving. I was and always am a minister, one who ministers to another. There are many ways to express this calling. I do not see rigidness, closed-mindedness, or tunnel vision as a friend. I do not live in a box; I do not even know where the box is. I hope I have been and continue to be open to seeing God in every experience, no matter where that may bring me.

As in the beginning and now at the end of this offering, I hope these experiences influence you to know there is a loving, unchanging Creator energy filled with tremendous good, just for you. You are part of it, it is part of you. There is no separation. May you begin to see the mystical of life, the magic in the universe, and the innate Divinity we are all created from. May you recognize your extraordinary moments, and learn to trust them. If you are not satisfied with your life, may you be willing to change your perceptions, to change your stories, and ultimately to change your life.

◆ ◆ ◆

◆ ◆ ◆

The outer learning is the way in,
the inner awareness is the way through.
Blessings upon your journey to yourself and
to God the good of a thousand names.
With great love, the end.

~ Deborah Evans Hogan

◆ ◆ ◆

ACKNOWLEDGMENTS

My gratitude to God the Creator, this immense yet immeasurable somethingness which is in all-ways present, that pushes me, provides for me, and made this book possible. Nothing exists without you. So, thank you for *all* of it! To my brother, friend, and way-shower, Jesus, "thank you" is simply not enough. The immensity of your love is beyond worldly comprehension.

To Reverend Shipley Allinson, thank you for seeing me. To Layne Cargill, who showed me what I did not even fathom was possible. To multiple authors, teachers, and speakers who have shared and do share their authentic hearts with us and have deeply affected my journey, thank you.

To every single client, Beloved, student, and congregant of my ministry and private practice, thank you. I love you. I would not be me without you. If you could feel my gratitude for you, for letting me in, for trusting me, for saying yes, for allowing me to witness you, you would burst open with so much Divine radiance you could not even speak.

To Irene Tomkinson, Spiritual Life Coach extraordinaire who was the first person to set eyes upon the very first draft, thank you for every single one of your holy scribbles! Your insights and questions changed, added, dug in, and caused hours of even more emotional excavation than I considered possible. Uncomfortable, yes. As always, deeply rewarding.

To my editor, Kate Victory Hannisian of Blue Pencil Consulting. The Divine kismet that drew us together is pure magic. As I write this acknowledgment we have yet to meet in person, and still, I know I can call you to whine. Your gentle manner is your superpower. Immense appreciation for your patience with my fire, as well as my first-time author personality. To book designer Robin Wrighton, I thank you for your ability to hear me and your talent to make my desires come to life on paper. As of this writing, I have great confidence with the yet-unfinished product! To Michelle Gold Mombrinie, photographer, I look forward to more collaborations. Your generous heart has been a gift to me and the readers of this book. Thank you.

To my friend Katherine T. Perrin, our laughter, rants, open hearts, and listening ears are high on my list of blessings. Being here for one another is a privilege. To Cynthia Rozzi, my city mouse sister, I love how our friendship never wanes. Marty Jacobus and Sue Chickering, thank you for your authenticity and for speaking my language. To Ganga-Mel and the sweet, sweet, cherished sacred somethingness between us, immense gratitude. To my Goddess circle of the '90s and into the great beyond, in body and no longer, you each have space in my thankful heart of Divine Love, laughter, life, and sharing of multidimensional possibilities. To the many strong and feisty women in my birth family who came before me and whose blood runs through my veins, thank you.

To my birth family; parents, siblings, relatives, and my family of choice, those who I call a friend and have called a friend, thank you for pushing me, loving me, accepting and not accepting me, for good comes from it all. Every moment is part of my tapestry, part of who I am. I would not be me without you. To Pamela Furlong, my appreciation for us joining one another on this journey is beyond my human comprehension. I look forward to finding out one day!

To my son, who always amazes me. Believe it or not, you are my inspiration. Your brilliant linear mind and massive feeling heart astonish me. Thank you once again, for choosing me as your parent. There are many times I wish I had "done better" for you, yet I have to trust I did the best I could in those moments, and the rest is up to you. I know you can accomplish anything you want.

You are a master manifester; manifest the positive, dear one. Remember, use your power for good. I love you beyond words.

Language cannot translate the massive tenderness my heart exudes in gratitude for my husband and favorite person, William Dalton Hogan, Jr. Bill expresses the epitome of Divine Okay-ness. When I rant, he calms. When I tense, he makes fun. When I struggle, he finds just the perfect word for me to have greater clarity. When I said to him, "I need time off from my practice to finish my book, I cannot figure out how to do that, how to make it work," he casually suggested, "so take a sabbatical." Okay, done.

Bill and I are very much the opposite, yet, as he says, we agree on the important things. He has described himself as the most irreverent person he knows. I describe him as the kindest person I know. Where I am very serious, Bill is very light. Where I am direct, Bill is middle-road gray. Where I am intense, Bill has left the room. Where Bill is grounded, solid and stable, I fly from here to there, constantly creating as the wheels in my mind turn and my heart directs. Yet, somehow, through loving, liking, and caring for one another and consciously choosing this life together, we manage to meet in the middle. We balance one another's extremes. This has been a bumpy road. It also has had smooth spots. Now, after twenty-eight years together, it is very sweet. I am grateful for us, for having found one another, again and again, staying again and again, and coming back again and again. You have helped to make me a better person, a nicer woman. I love you. Thank you, to the other half of my ministry, the stable breadwinner with a real job, the one without whom all this would never have been possible. Your unconditional support of me and my calling knows no boundaries.

◆ ◆ ◆

Prepare your mind to receive
the best that life has to offer.

~ Dr. Ernest Holmes

◆ ◆ ◆

SUGGESTED AUTHORS & READING LIST

Lynn V. Andrews. *Tree of Dreams: A Spirit Woman's Vision of Transition and Change* (2001), *Woman at the Edge of Two Worlds* (1994), *Windhorse Woman: A Marriage of Spirit* (1990), and *Star Woman: We Are Made from Stars and to the Stars We Must Return* (1987). See www.lynnandrews.com.

Hilda Charlton. *Saints Alive* (1989). See www.HildaCharlton.com.

Paul Ferrini. My favorites include *Love Without Conditions* (1994) and *Reflections of the Christ Mind* (2000). See www.lightforthesoul.com.

Dr. Ernest Holmes. Founder of Science of Mind. See www.csl.org. and www.new-thought-center.com.

Charles and Myrtle Filmore. Founders of Unity. See www.unity.org.

Emma Cutis Hopkins. *High Mysticism: A Series of Twelve Studies in the Wisdom of the Sages of the Ages* (1920). See www.emmacurtishopkins.com.

Joel S. Goldsmith. *The Infinite Way* (1947) and many other books. See www.joelgoldsmith.com.

Osho. Find out more about the writings of Osho at www.osho.com.

Neale Donald Walsch. *Conversations with God* series (4 primary books plus more). See www.nealedonaldwalsch.com.

◆ ◆ ◆

If you love a flower, don't pick it up.
Because if you pick it up it dies
and it ceases to be what you love.

So, if you love a flower,
let it be.

Love is not about possession.
Love is about appreciation.

~ Osho

◆ ◆ ◆

ABOUT THE AUTHOR

DEBORAH EVANS HOGAN, born in Haverhill, Massachusetts at what the locals now call the "old Hale Hospital," has strong New England roots. Much to her mother's dismay, she failed the test to be accepted into a "proper" private school for first grade because when asked to draw as many straight lines as she could in a timed minute, Deborah asked for a ruler. The only child who did. Wrong. You failed. Good bye. Since that moment, Deborah knew she was not like the others. A born empath, each day of public school first grade she would come home and immediately go to bed, sleeping through the night. The outer world was not comfortable for her yet-unclaimed heightened sensibilities. She lived in the northeast, always within half an hour of where she was born, until, at the age of sixty, she and her husband moved to the Nashoba Valley region of Massachusetts. Deborah has taken up residence as the crazy lady in the woods. *Mystical Partnership* is her first official "real" book. Her first attempt, a self-published spiral-bound uniquely small book called *Simple Steps to Clarity* (which she bought up all random copies off of Amazon prior to completing this manuscript), was not a big hit.

Deborah has always taken the road less travelled, and it suits her. Ordained as an interfaith minister in 1997, Deborah goes where Spirit calls her, whether that is guest speaking, proprietor of four healing centers, an on-line ministry, nine years in church ministry, a private healing and counseling practice for over 30 years, and a successful cable television show, *Your Alternative Health Choices.* Deborah's path has appeared varied, yet she has always been led through her faith in the Divine Architect in order to witness the mystical of life revealed.

For more information visit, www.amethystlight.org or on Facebook with Deborah Evans Hogan of The Amethyst Light Ministry.

◆ ◆ ◆

You cannot experience joy in life by
opposing the ideas or actions of other people.
You can experience joy only by remaining
faithful to the truth within your own heart.
And this truth never rejects others,
but invites them in.

~ Paul Ferrini, "Love Without Conditions"

◆ ◆ ◆